SPECTRUM®

Test Prep

Grade 1

Published by Spectrum®
An imprint of Carson-Dellosa Publishing LLC
Greensboro, North Carolina

An imprint of Carson-Dellosa Publishing LLC
P.O. Box 35665
Greensboro, NC 27425 USA

ISBN 978-1-4838-1372-1

01-349147811

Table of Contents

What's Inside?

Spectrum® Test Prep is designed to help you and your first grader prepare and plan for success on standardized tests.

Strategies

This workbook is structured around strategies. A strategy is a careful plan or method for achieving a particular goal, such as succeeding on a test. Strategies can be broad general strategies about a test as a whole or a category of skills. Strategies can also be specific, providing step-by-step instructions on how to tackle a problem or offering guidelines on how to answer a question about a story. Learning how to apply a strategy gives test-takers a plan for how to approach a test as a whole and how to answer questions.

This workbook offers a set of broad strategies as well as very specific strategies. General test-taking strategies apply to all tests, and should be used to help prepare for the test. Specific strategies for English Language Arts and Mathematics tests are divided into larger categories of skills students will encounter, such as reading literature or performing calculations. On each practice page, you will find even more specific strategies that apply to the skills.

Test Tips

Test Tips are included throughout the practice pages. While strategies offer a plan for answering test items, Test Tips offer ideas for how to apply each strategy or how to approach a type of question. There are general Test Tips that apply to all tests as well as specific Test Tips for English Language Arts and Mathematics tests.

Practice Pages

This workbook is divided into two sections, English Language Arts and Mathematics. Each section has practice activities that have questions similar to those that will appear on standardized tests. Also included are strategies and Test Tips to guide students. Students should use a pencil to complete these activities.

Strategy Review Pages

Strategy review pages give your student an opportunity to review and practice important strategies in each content area. These strategies cover the important skills students will encounter on tests in English Language Arts and Mathematics.

Answer Key

Answers for all of the practice pages and strategy review pages are found in an answer key at the end of the book.

Test-Taking Strategies

Being prepared is key to doing your best on test day. Read the tips below to help you prepare for tests.

In the days before the test...

- Keep up on your reading, worksheets, and assignments. Completing all your assigned work will help you be better prepared for the test.

- Don't wait until right before the test to review materials. Create a study schedule for the best result. That way, you can study a bit at a time and not all at once.

- Take advantage of sample items and practice tests. Complete these to practice for your test. If you run into concepts or skills that are new, ask a teacher or other adult.

The night before the test...

- Don't try to study everything all over again the night before. If you've been studying in the days before the test, all you need the night before is a light review of your notes. Remind yourself of the key ideas and practice a few skills, but don't study late into the night.

- Make sure you have all the materials you will need for the test, such as pencils, paper, and a calculator. Check with your teacher to make sure you know what tools to bring. Having everything ready the night before will make the morning less stressful.

- Get a good night's sleep the night before the test. If you are well rested, you will be more alert and able to do your best.

On the day of the test...

- Don't skip breakfast. If you are hungry, you won't be thinking about the test. You'll be thinking about lunch.

- Make sure you have at least two sharpened pencils with you and any other tools needed.

- Read all directions carefully. Make sure you understand how you are supposed to answer each question.

- For multiple choice questions, read all the possible answers before choosing one. If you know that some answers are wrong, cross them off. Even if you have to guess, this will eliminate some wrong answers.

- Once you choose or write an answer, double check it by reading the question again. Confirm that your answer is correct.

- Answer every part of a question. If a question asks you to show your work or to explain how you arrived at an answer, make sure you include that information.

- If you are stuck on a question, or unsure, mark it lightly with a pencil and move on. If you have time, you can come back. This is especially true on a timed test.

- Breathe! Remind yourself that you've prepared for the test and that you will do your best!

Strategies for English Language Arts Tests

Read the strategies below to learn more about how they work.

Use details from a story or passage to show your understanding.
Authors choose details to include in their writing. Every detail is important. As you read, look for details. Think about why the author chose those details. Use them to understand what the author means.

Use details to make a picture in your mind as you read.
Authors use descriptive details to paint a picture for readers. As you read, try to picture in your mind what people, places, and events look like.

Look carefully at pictures.
Authors include pictures, photos, and text features like charts and webs to show something about the words on the page. As you read, use them to help you understand what you are reading.

Reread to answer questions.
If you don't know the answer to a question right away, don't worry! You can go back and read the story or passage again. As you reread, look for the answer to the question.

Ask questions as you read.
Careful readers stop once in a while to think about what they are reading. They ask questions like, *What was this paragraph about?* As you read, ask yourself questions to make sure you understand.

Pay attention to how parts of a story or passage connect and fit together.
Authors work hard to make sure the parts of their writing fit together. In a story, the characters, place, and events fit together. In nonfiction, authors usually keep connected ideas together.

When you write, use details to support main ideas.
If you write a story, include details that help the reader see, smell, and hear the characters, places, and events. If you write nonfiction, use details to support a main idea.

Plan your writing.
Make a plan before you start writing. For stories, make sure you choose characters, a setting, and events. Your story should have a beginning, middle, and end. For nonfiction, choose main ideas. Usually one to three main ideas is enough. Then, support each main idea with details that help explain.

Revise to make sure your writing makes sense. Then, edit to fix errors. Use what you know about nouns, verbs, adjectives, and adverbs to make correct choices when you edit.
After you finish your draft, you may have time to revise and edit. First, revise to make sure your words say what you want them to say. Then, check spelling, capitalization, punctuation, and grammar to catch and fix errors.

English Language Arts

Describe Story Elements
Reading: Literature

DIRECTIONS: Read the story. Then, answer the questions using details from the story.

> **The New Puppy**
> My name is Matt. Today is my birthday. I am seven years old. I asked my mom and dad for a puppy for my birthday. They told me I am too little to take care of a puppy. But I think I can do it. I can walk the puppy. I can feed the puppy. I can love the puppy. I hope I get a puppy today!
> The house is ready for Matt's birthday party. There are red, yellow, and blue balloons. There are streamers. There is a sign that says, "HAPPY BIRTHDAY, MATT!" I am Matt's mom. Matt is so excited for his birthday. All of his friends and family are here. We will have a great time.
> "Matt! It is time to open your gifts!" I call over the music. Matt comes running into the room. He is smiling. He is excited. He opens all of his gifts. He gets a new racecar. He gets a new sweater. He did not get a puppy. "Mom, is there anything else?" he asks me. Just then, Matt's dad comes in the room. He has a blue leash in his hand. There is a puppy at the end of the leash. "Happy Birthday, Matt!" we both say. The puppy barks.

Strategy
As you read, identify the story parts—the characters, where the characters are, and what the characters do.

Test Tip
Stories have characters, setting, and events. Characters are the people or animals in the story. The setting is where the story takes place. Events are what happens to characters.

1. **Who is having a birthday in the story?**
   - (A) Matt's mom
   - (B) Matt's dad
   - (C) Matt
   - (D) Matt's puppy

   Write how you know.

   _____

   _____

   _____

2. **Write the key detail that tells where Matt is having his birthday party.**

   _____

   _____

3. **Who is telling the story at the beginning?**

   _____

   Write how you know.

   _____

   _____

4. **Write a question that uses the key detail "All of his friends and family are here."**

   _____

   _____

   _____

Describe Story Elements
Reading: Literature

DIRECTIONS: Read the story. Then, answer the questions using details from the story.

adapted from *The Tale of Peter Rabbit*
by Beatrix Potter

Once upon a time there were four little rabbits. Their names were Flopsy, Mopsy, Cotton–tail, and Peter. They lived with their mother. They lived under the root of a very big fir tree.

One morning, Mrs. Rabbit said, "You may go into the fields. You may go down the lane. But don't go into Mr. McGregor's garden. Your father had an accident there. He was put in a pie by Mrs. McGregor."

"Now run along. And don't get into trouble. I am going out."

Then, Mrs. Rabbit took a basket and her umbrella. She went through the woods to the baker's. She bought a loaf of brown bread and five raisin buns.

Flopsy, Mopsy, and Cotton–tail were good little bunnies. They went down the lane to gather berries. But Peter was very naughty. He ran straight away to Mr. McGregor's garden. He squeezed under the gate!

Strategy | Read the story carefully. Then, retell the story to yourself to make sure you understand it.

Test Tip | To find the events in a story, ask yourself what happens to the characters.

5. **Who is this story about?**

   (A) four foxes and their mother

   (B) four rabbits and their mother

   (C) Mr. McGregor and his wife

   (D) a baker

6. **Write the key details that helped you answer the question above.**

   _____

   _____

   _____

   _____

7. **Write a key detail that tells what happened to the rabbits' father.**

   _____

8. **Write a question that uses the detail, "She bought a loaf of brown bread and five raisin buns."**

   _____

   _____

9. **Where did Flopsy, Mopsy, and Cotton–tail go?**

   (A) to the baker's

   (B) down the lane to gather berries

   (C) to Mr. McGregor's garden

   (D) to visit Mrs. McGregor

10. **What is the setting of this story?**

   (A) in the city

   (B) in the country

   (C) under a tree

   (D) in the woods

Name _____ Date _____

English Language Arts

Identify Sensory Words
Reading: Literature

DIRECTIONS: Read the sentences. Then, answer the questions.

EXAMPLE

The cat sleeps. His fur is soft. He purrs loudly.

Which word tells what sound the cat is making?

(A) sleeps

(B) soft

● purrs

(D) cat

1. **The sun is hot. The clouds are puffy. The wind blows softly. I see a bird fly.**

   Which sentences tell what you can see?

   (A) The sun is hot.

   (B) The clouds are puffy.

   (C) The wind blows softly.

   (D) I see a bird fly.

   Write how you know.

   _____

   _____

2. **Mom grows roses in the yard. The petals are big and red. Be careful with the stems. They are prickly!**

   Write the words that describe using senses.

   _____

Which senses do the words tell about?

_____

What other sense might tell about roses?

_____

3. **If a character was smiling and laughing while dancing on the beach, she feels _____.**

4. **Write the detail that helps you answer the question above.**

   _____

5. **Choose the sentence that uses words that tell about feeling excited.**

   (A) A dog walks slowly in the woods.

   (B) A blue fish jumps out of the water.

   (C) The horse dashes like lightning down the lane.

   (D) The ball rolls on the grass.

   Write the words that show feeling excited.

   _____

   _____

Identify Sensory Words
Reading: Literature

DIRECTIONS: Read the words that tell about the senses. Then, answer the questions.

Strategy Categorize words, or put words that go together, into groups.

Test Tip Authors use words to tell, or to describe. As you read, picture in your mind what a word is describing. Use all of your senses.

EXAMPLE

Read the list. Then, write the words that tell about something cozy.

hard chair	Things that are <u>cozy</u>:
warm oven	1. soft bed
soft bed	2. thick blanket
stairs	
thick blanket	

6. Write the words that tell about something that has a loud sound in the sentence below.

The fire truck screamed, its booming siren filling the street with noise.

_____

_____

7. **Read the list. Then, write the words that tell about something hot.**

ice cream
soup
crackers
oatmeal
fruit
Foods that are <u>hot</u>:
1.
2.

DIRECTIONS: Read the story. Then, answer the questions about the words in the story.

The rocket ship was <u>big</u>. It was as tall as a skyscraper! The engines <u>started</u>. The countdown began. The rocket flew up into the sky.

8. **Choose two words that tell about the size of the rocket ship.**

(A) large

(B) gigantic

(C) small

(D) tiny

Explain why the word *gigantic* is a better word to use than big.

_____

_____

9. **Which tells about the sound the rocket might make when it started?**

(A) shut down

(B) ended

(C) whispered

(D) roared

Which two sentences show that *roared* might be a better word to use than *started*?

(A) It describes the sound the engines make.

(B) It paints a picture in the reader's mind.

(C) It means the same thing.

(D) It is not a better word.

English Language Arts

Identify Characters and Theme
Reading: Literature

DIRECTIONS: Continue reading from *The Tale of Peter Rabbit*. Then, answer the questions using details from the story.

> Flopsy, Mopsy, and Cotton-tail listened to Mother. They did not go into Mr. McGregor's garden. They went to gather berries. But Peter ran to Mr. McGregor's garden and squeezed under the gate.
>
> First he ate some lettuce and beans. Then, he ate some radishes. After that, he felt rather sick. So he went to look for some parsley.
> But at the end of a cucumber frame, he met Mr. McGregor!
> Mr. McGregor was on his hands and knees planting cabbages. He jumped up and ran after Peter. He waved a rake and called, "Stop thief!"
> Peter was very scared. He rushed all over the garden. He had forgotten the way back to the gate!
> He lost one of his shoes in the cabbages. He lost the other shoe in the potatoes.
> After losing them, he ran on four legs and went faster. He may have gotten away if he had not run into a net and got caught by the large buttons on his jacket. It was a new blue jacket with brass buttons.

Strategy   As you read, find details about how characters are alike and how they are different.

Test Tip   Events are what happens to characters. Stories can have many characters. Make a list to help you remember them.

1. **These events from the story are out of order. Write the numbers 2, 3, 4, 5, and 6 to retell *The Tale of Peter Rabbit*.**

   ☐ Peter eats lettuce and beans and radishes.

   ☐ Peter forgets his way back to the gate.

   ☐ Peter runs and loses his shoes.

   ☐ Peter goes into Mr. McGregor's garden.

   ☐ Mr. McGregor sees Peter in his garden.

   ☐ Peter gets caught in a net.

   Write how you know.

   _____

   _____

2. **How is Peter different from the other bunnies?**

   (A) He is good and they are naughty.

   (B) He is white and they are brown.

   (C) He is fat and they are thin.

   (D) He is naughty and they are good.

   Write how you know.

   _____

   _____

3. **Choose the key detail that tells why Peter went to look for parsley.**

   (A) "After that, he felt rather sick."

   (B) "Mr. McGregor was on his hands and knees planting cabbages."

   (C) "Peter was very scared."

   (D) "He lost one of his shoes in the cabbages."

English Language Arts

Identify Characters and Theme
Reading: Literature

DIRECTIONS: Finish reading *The Tale of Peter Rabbit*. Then, answer the questions using details from the story.

Peter was trapped in the net in Mr. McGregor's garden. Mr. McGregor was getting closer...
Peter gave up and began to cry. Some friendly birds flew to him. They begged him not to give up. Mr. McGregor tried to pop a bowl over Peter. Peter wriggled out just in time, leaving his jacket behind him.

Peter rushed into the tool shed. He jumped into a can. Mr. McGregor was sure that Peter was in the tool shed. He began to look under flowerpots. Suddenly Peter sneezed—'AH–choo!' Mr. McGregor was after him in no time. Peter jumped out of a window. The window was too small for Mr. McGregor, and he was tired of running after Peter. He went back to his work.

Peter sat down to rest. He was out of breath and shaking with fright. He had no idea which way to go. Soon he began to wander around. He climbed up on a wheelbarrow. The first thing he saw was Mr. McGregor. His back was turned towards Peter. Beyond him was the gate!

Peter got down very quietly. He started running as fast as he could go. Mr. McGregor saw him at the corner. Peter slipped underneath the gate. He was safe at last in the woods outside the garden. Peter did not stop running or look behind him until he got home. He flopped down on the nice soft sand on the floor of the rabbit–hole and shut his eyes. His mother put him to bed and made him some tea. But Flopsy, Mopsy, and Cotton–tail had bread and milk and berries for supper.

Strategy
Look for details that tell how characters' choices make events happen. Characters may choose to act a certain way. For example, Peter chooses to go into the garden.

4. Write two things you know about Mr. McGregor from this story

_____

_____

5. Put a checkmark (✓) in each box to show which character the words describe.

	Peter Rabbit	Mr. McGregor	Flopsy, Mopsy, and Cotton–tail
Works hard in the garden			
Lives under a tree			
Did not listen to Mrs. Rabbit			
Picked berries			
Chased Peter			
Only got tea for supper			
Had bread, milk, and berries for supper			

6. The story says that "Peter gave up and began to cry." Which two sentences from the story tell you why Peter decided not to give up?

(A) "Peter gave up and began to cry."

(B) "Peter sat down to rest."

(C) "Some friendly birds flew to him."

(D) "They begged him not to give up."

7. Mr. McGregor stops chasing Peter. What does this tell you about him? Use a detail from the story.

_____

_____

_____

English Language Arts

Contrast Fiction and Nonfiction
Reading: Informational Text

DIRECTIONS: Read the story. Then, answer the questions using details from the story.

Bertie the Cow

Bertie the cow lived on a farm. She lived with chickens and pigs and horses. Bertie liked living on the farm. Every day, Farmer Joe fed her fresh, green grass. Every day, Farmer Joe gave her cool, clean water. It was a good life for a cow. One day, Farmer Joe came into the barn. He tied a rope around Bertie's neck. He led her out of the barn. He put Bertie in a truck. They drove a long, long way.

Finally, the truck stopped. Farmer Joe took Bertie out of the truck. She looked around. There were many animals. There were cows and pigs and horses. But this was not a farm. This was a fair! Bertie had heard about the fair. She knew that animals went to the fair and came home with pretty ribbons. Bertie wanted a pretty ribbon. She held her head high. She fluffed her tail.

Many people came to look at Bertie. She heard words like "lovely" and "strong" and "healthy." Bertie mooed softly for the people. Bertie swished her tail for the people. Finally, at the end of the day, Farmer Joe came back to Bertie. He had a pretty blue ribbon in his hand. Bertie felt very proud!

Strategy — As you read, ask yourself questions to identify characters, setting, and events: *Who is the story about? Where do the events take place? What happens?*

Test Tip — As you read, remember that stories are made up and can't happen in real life.

1. Who are the characters in the story?

_____

_____

2. Is Bertie a real cow? _____

Which two sentences from the story helped you answer the question above?

(A) "Bertie the cow lived on a farm."

(B) "Farmer Joe took Bertie out of the truck."

(C) "Bertie wanted a pretty ribbon."

(D) "Bertie felt very proud!"

3. Write why Farmer Joe took Bertie to the fair.

_____

_____

4. Choose two sentences that show "It was a good life for a cow."

(A) "She lived with chickens and pigs and horses."

(B) "Every day, Farmer Joe fed her fresh, green grass."

(C) "Every day, Farmer Joe gave her cool, clean water."

(D) "Bertie the cow lived on a farm."

5. Write a sentence that shows the setting.

_____

6. Is "Bertie the Cow" a story or a passage that gives information? How do you know?

_____

_____

_____

English Language Arts

Contrast Fiction and Nonfiction
Reading: Informational Text

DIRECTIONS: Read the passage. Then, answer the questions using details from the passage.

Prize-Winning Cows

Cows are interesting animals. Dairy cows give us milk. Milk comes from a cow's udder. The udder can hold up to 50 pounds of milk. That is as heavy as a young child! Some people think that cows have many stomachs. They really only have one stomach. But it has four parts. These four parts help the cow eat hay and grass.

Many children around the world raise dairy cows. These children take care of their cows. They feed them. They give them water. They brush their coats. They clean their hooves. They milk them. And, they enter them in shows. Children can win prizes for having the best dairy cow.

How can a dairy cow win prizes? Each cow gets points. Judges look at the cow's udder to make sure it is easy to milk. They see how big the cow is. It cannot be too fat or too thin. They make sure the cow is healthy and can make milk. Children who win prizes for their dairy cows are very proud. They worked hard!

Strategy Reread both the story "Bertie the Cow" and the passage "Prize–Winning Cows" and list ways that they are alike and different.

Test Tip A passage gives information and facts about a topic. Passages do not have characters, but they do tell about people, animals, and events in the world.

7. **What information is given in the passage "Prize–Winning Cows"?**

(A) reasons that cows are interesting

(B) details about county fairs

(C) facts about dairy farms

(D) events about Bertie the cow

8. **Which sentence tells about the passage "Prize–Winning Cows"?**

(A) a story that gives information

(B) a fairy tale

(C) a story that teaches a lesson

(D) a poem about animals

Write how you know.

_____

_____

9. **Write one key detail that tells why cows are interesting.**

_____

_____

10. **Write two key details that show how Bertie is like a real cow.**

_____

_____

11. **How are these two stories different?**

(A) "Bertie the Cow" gives information and "Prize–Winning Cows" tells a story.

(B) "Bertie the Cow" has facts and "Prize–Winning Cows" does not.

(C) "Bertie the Cow" tells a story and "Prize–Winning Cows" gives information.

(D) "Bertie the Cow" is real and "Prize–Winning Cows" is made up.

Use Key Details
Reading: Informational Text

DIRECTIONS: Read the passage. Then, answer the questions using key details from the passage.

Spiders
Spiders are animals. All spiders have eight legs. Most spiders spin webs of silk. The webs help the spiders catch food. They eat mostly insects.

Some spiders are <u>gigantic</u>. There is one as big as a man's hand. Other spiders are very small. One spider is as small as the tip of a pin.

Strategy — To find key details, look for sentences that answer questions that begin with *who, what, where, when,* and *why.*

Test Tip — When reading a passage, find the details that tell what the passage is mostly about.

1. Spiders are _____.

   Write how you know.

   _____

   _____

2. Which sentence helps you know the meaning of the word gigantic? What is the meaning?

   _____

   _____

3. Write two key details that give facts about what spiders look like.

   _____

   _____

   _____

4. What are spider webs made of?
   - (A) silk
   - (B) rope
   - (C) wire
   - (D) metal

   Write how you know.

   _____

   _____

5. Which key detail tells you why spiders spin webs?
   - (A) "Spiders are animals."
   - (B) "The webs help the spiders catch food."
   - (C) "They eat mostly insects."
   - (D) "One spider is as small as the tip of a pin."

6. Write a question that uses the key detail "They eat mostly insects."

   _____

   _____

7. Which key detail would not fit with this passage?
   - (A) Anna and David are afraid of spiders.
   - (B) Spiders often trap flies in their webs.
   - (C) The webs spiders spin have many patterns.
   - (D) Some spiders live in the ground.

English Language Arts

Use Key Details
Reading: Informational Text

DIRECTIONS: Read the passage. Then, answer the questions using key details from the passage.

Rabbits

Rabbits are small animals. They have fluffy tails. Some rabbits have long ears so they can hear very well. Some rabbits have floppy ears. Others stick right up!

Rabbits eat all kinds of plants. They eat in fields. They eat in gardens. Some farmers do not like rabbits. They eat the vegetables the farmers grow.

Some people have pet rabbits. They keep them in <u>pens</u>, or cages. Vegetables and grass are good foods for rabbits.

Strategy Make a list of details to help you understand what you read. Here, you can make a list of details about rabbits.

Test Tip <u>Underlined</u>, **bold**, and *italicized* words are important.

8. **What is the passage mostly about?**
   - (A) plants rabbits eat
   - (B) farming
   - (C) vegetables
   - (D) rabbits

   Write how you know.

   _____

   _____

9. **Why do some farmers not like rabbits?**
   - (A) They run on the grass.
   - (B) They eat the vegetables the farmers grow.
   - (C) They make too much noise.
   - (D) They have fluffy tails.

10. **Write the key detail that tells about good foods for rabbits.**

    _____

    _____

11. **What words or phrases help you find the meaning of the word *pens*?**

    _____

    _____

12. **Write a question that uses the key detail that rabbits are small animals.**

    _____

    _____

13. **Which detail would be good to add to this passage?**
    - (A) what rabbits eat
    - (B) how to care for a pet rabbit
    - (C) why farmers love rabbits
    - (D) types of dogs and cats

Use Main Idea and Details
Reading: Informational Text

DIRECTIONS: Read the passage. Then, answer the questions using details from the passage.

> **Sign Language**
> People who cannot hear well use sign language. Some people use sign language because they cannot speak well. They use their hands to talk. Their hands make signals. The signals show letters. The signals show words and ideas.
> Other people use sign language, too. Have you ever watched a sports game? Players use their hands. They make signs to tell each other where to go. Have you ever been stuck in a traffic jam? A police officer can use sign language to tell cars to go and to stop.
> Even you use sign language. You wave your hand to say hello and to say good–bye. You use your fingers to point. You use your fingers to show which way to go. We use our hands to make signals all of the time!

Strategy To find the main idea, ask yourself *What is this passage mostly about?*

Test Tip The main topic is what the whole passage is about. The main topic may be written at the beginning or the end of the passage.

1. **What is the main topic of the passage?**

   Ⓐ "People who cannot hear well use sign language."

   Ⓑ "Players use their hands."

   Ⓒ "Even you use sign language."

   Ⓓ "We use our hands to make signals all of the time!"

Test Tip

Passages give information, or ideas. Words like *and, because, so,* and *since* connect two ideas. For example, *The car did not run because it was out of gas*.

2. **Write the word that connects two ideas in the sentence below.**

   You wave your hand to say hello and to say good–bye.

   _____

3. **Write two ways that you use sign language every day.**

   _____

   _____

4. **What do people use to make signals?**

   Ⓐ their hands and arms

   Ⓑ their eyes, ears, and mouth

   Ⓒ their feet and toes

   Ⓓ their hair and head

   Write the key detail that helped you answer the question above.

   _____

5. **Read the sentence.**

   Some people use sign language because they cannot speak well.

   Which word is used to show the reason that some people use sign language?

   _____

Use Main Idea and Details
Reading: Informational Text

DIRECTIONS: Read the passage. Then, answer the questions using details from the passage.

> **Apples**
>
> Apples need all four seasons to grow. Apple trees grow white flowers in the spring. They grow small green leaves. Then, the flowers drop off. Tiny green apples start to grow.
>
> Tree branches fill with small apples in the summer. Big apples are ready to be picked in the fall. Leaves start to fall off the branches.
>
> The apple tree will rest in the winter. It does not grow any leaves. It does not grow any apples. It gets ready for the spring.

Strategy   As you read, look for details that tell about the main topic.

6. **What is the main topic of this passage?**

   (A) Apples need all four seasons to grow.

   (B) Apple trees grow white flowers in the spring.

   (C) The branches fill with small apples in the summer.

   (D) Big apples are ready to be picked in the fall.

7. **Write three key details that tell more about the main topic.**

Main topic	Apples need all four seasons to grow
Key detail	
Key detail	
Key detail	

8. **What happens to apple trees in the winter?**

   (A) They grow taller.

   (B) They rest for a few months.

   (C) They lose their branches.

   (D) They fall over in the snow.

Which key detail helped you answer the question?

   (A) "Apple trees grow white flowers in the spring."

   (B) "Tree branches fill with small apples in the summer."

   (C) "Big apples are ready to be picked in the fall."

   (D) "The apple tree will rest in the winter."

9. **Read the sentence below.**

   Apple trees do not grow apples in the winter because they are getting ready for the spring.

   Which word is used to show the reason that apple trees do not grow in winter?

   _____

10. **What information could you add to this passage?**

   (A) different types of apples

   (B) the weather in each season

   (C) kinds of flowers

   (D) picking apples in fall

11. **Which sentence tells why the seasons are included in this passage?**

   _____

   _____

English Language Arts

Determine Meaning
Reading: Informational Text

DIRECTIONS: Read the question and answer choices. Choose the best answer.

Strategy — Use the other words in the sentence to find out which word to use. The other words in the sentence are clues.

Test Tip — Ask yourself questions about the missing word. For example, read this sentence.
Anna added _____ to her cereal at breakfast.
You can ask yourself, What do people add to cereal? (milk)

1. **The bee flew to its _____. It went inside.**
   - (A) corner
   - (B) cup
   - (C) hive
   - (D) honey

   Write a question that would help you find the answer for the question above.

   _____

   _____

Test Tip — Use word parts to help you with the meaning of words. For example, the word part *re–* means "again." So, the meaning of replay is "to play again."

2. **Harry _____ his shoes before taking them off.**
   - (A) tying
   - (B) unties
   - (C) reties
   - (D) tied

   Write how you know.

   _____

   _____

   _____

3. **I reread that book three times.**

   What does the word reread mean?
   - (A) read one time
   - (B) read first
   - (C) read again
   - (D) did not read

Test Tip — You can also look for the root word in words to find meaning. The words cooks, cooked, and cooking all have the same root word—cook.

4. **Sara <u>looks</u> at the painting for a long time.**

   What is the root word of the underlined word?

   _____

5. **Pia is <u>sing</u> at the party tonight.**

   Which word has the ending that makes sense for the underlined word?
   - (A) sings
   - (B) singed
   - (C) singing
   - (D) singer

English Language Arts

Use Text Features
Reading: Informational Text

DIRECTIONS: Read the question and answer choices. Choose the best answer.

Strategy — Use information in charts, lists, and pictures to help you understand a passage.

Test Tip — Many passages that give information include the following text features:
- table of contents: tells what page a topic or chapter starts on
- glossary: gives the meanings of words in the passage
- headings: titles of paragraphs

1. **Read the table of contents below. Which chapter tells about making shoes?**

Table of Contents	
Chapter 1—The Shoe Store	2
Chapter 2—Kinds of Shoes	4
Chapter 3—Making Shoes	8
Chapter 4—Selling Shoes	10

- (A) 1
- (B) 2
- (C) 3
- (D) 4

2. **On what page does the chapter about making shoes start?**
- (A) 2
- (B) 4
- (C) 8
- (D) 10

3. **Read the glossary below.**

GLOSSARY	
Flower	the part of a plant that is colorful; the seeds of the plant are in the flower
Plant	to put a seed or flower into the ground to grow
Root	the part of a plant or flower that is in the ground; it gets food and water for the plant
Seed	a small object made by a plant that grows a new plant
Stem	a part of a plant that holds another part

What is a root?
- (A) the part of a plant that is colorful
- (B) to put a seed or flower into the ground to grow
- (C) the part of a plant or flower that is in the ground
- (D) a small object made by a plant that grows a new plant

Which part of the plant holds the flower?

_____

_____

Write how you know.

_____

_____

Name _____ Date _____

Make Connections
Reading: Informational Text

DIRECTIONS: Read the passage. Then, answer the questions using details from the passage.

Strategy — Make connections by finding what is the same and what is different about people, things, events, or places in a passage.

Test Tip — As you read, look for details that show how the Fourth of July and Veterans Day are the same and how they are different.

American Holidays

We have many holidays in America. One fun holiday is the Fourth of July. Many people have parties on the Fourth of July. Many people watch fireworks shows. But why do we celebrate that day? The Fourth of July is the day we celebrate the birth of our country. America used to be ruled by England. A long time ago, soldiers fought for freedom. The Fourth of July is the day we celebrate that freedom.

Veterans Day is another important holiday. Veterans Day is a quieter holiday. It is the day to remember our soldiers. Soldiers fight to keep us free. They fight to keep us safe. The Fourth of July celebrates our freedom. Veterans Day celebrates the men and women who keep us free.

1. **Which key details tell you why the Fourth of July is an important holiday?**

   (A) "Many people have parties on the Fourth of July."

   (B) "Many people watch fireworks shows."

   (C) "The Fourth of July is the day we celebrate the birth of our country."

   (D) "America used to be ruled by England."

2. **What do we celebrate on Veterans Day?**

   _____

   Write the key detail that helped you answer the question above.

   _____

   _____

3. **What two ideas are connected in this passage?**

   _____

   _____

4. **Find 3 sentences in the passage that tell how the Fourth of July and Veterans Day are alike. Write the ideas in the graphic organizer.**

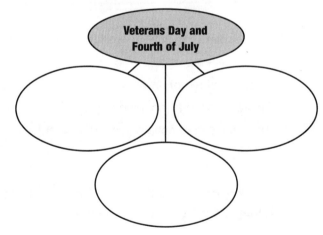

5. **Write how the Fourth of July and Veterans Day are different in your own words. Use details from the passage.**

   _____

   _____

   _____

Make Connections
Reading: Informational Text

DIRECTIONS: Read the passage. Then, answer the questions using details from the passage.

Strategy — As you read, make a list of ideas and people. Then, write how they are alike.

Test Tip — You can find details in the passage that connect firefighters and police officers—both people help others.

People Who Help

Firefighters are people who help. They work hard to keep us safe. They are very brave. Firefighters work long hours. Fires are very dangerous. Many firefighters get hurt in fires. Firefighters also help with traffic accidents. They make sure that all of the people around the accident stay safe.

Police officers are people who help, too. They keep us safe by making sure we follow the laws. If a person breaks the law, a police officer will take care of it. Police officers can also help if there is trouble. A police officer can help you if you are lost.

6. How are firefighters and police officers the same?

- (A) They both fight fires.
- (B) They both catch criminals.
- (C) They both ride in fire trucks.
- (D) They are both people who help.

7. Which key detail tells how firefighters help us?

- (A) Firefighters are people who help.
- (B) They not afraid of anything.
- (C) Firefighters work very long days.
- (D) They make sure people near an accident stay safe.

8. Write a key detail about police officers that shows how they are different from firefighters.

_____

_____

_____

9. Who would you call if someone took your bike?

_____

10. Who would you call to report a fire in the park?

_____

11. What other job would fit in this passage about people who help?

- (A) student
- (B) banker
- (C) nurse
- (D) baker

Name _____ Date _____

English Language Arts

Use Pictures
Reading: Informational Text

DIRECTIONS: Read the passage and look at the pictures. Then, answer the questions.

Strategy   Compare the information given in the passage and in the pictures.

Test Tip   Pictures and the words in the passage work together to give you all the information. Pictures may match the information in the passage. They may give more information to help you understand the passage.

EXAMPLE

     Rabbits are small animals. Some rabbits are brown. Some rabbits are black. Rabbits have fluffy tails. Some rabbits have long ears. Other rabbits have floppy ears.

Put a checkmark (✓) to show if the key detail came from the passage or from the picture.

	From passage	From picture
Rabbits are small animals.	✓	
Rabbits have whiskers.		✓
Some rabbits are brown.	✓	
Rabbits can sit on their hind legs.		✓

1. Ethan is tired. He had a busy day. He went fishing. He went swimming. He went hiking. Now he is sleeping.

Put a checkmark (✓) to show if the key detail came from the passage or from the picture.

	From passage	From picture
Ethan is tired.		
Ethan is camping.		
Ethan is in a tent.		
Ethan went swimming.		

2. Horses are big animals. They can be brown. They can be black. Horses are very strong.

What new information about horses is shown in the picture?

_____

3. Beth likes to go to the park. She likes to slide. She likes to jump.

Write a detail you learned from the passage and a detail you learned from the picture.

Passage

_____

_____

Picture

_____

_____

Use Pictures
Reading: Informational Text

DIRECTIONS: Read each passage carefully. Then, choose the best answer for the question.

Strategy | Ask yourself how the picture fits with the passage. What information does it give the reader?

Test Tip | Use the picture as well as the passage to answer the questions.

EXAMPLE

Monkeys are funny animals. They can use their tails to hang from trees. They use their hands just like we do. Monkeys like to play.

Why can monkeys use their tails to hang from trees?

● Their tails are long.

(B) Their tails are short.

(C) Their tails are sticky.

(D) Their tails have glue.

Write how you know.

The picture shows a monkey with a long tail.

4. **Gabe likes sports. Today, he is playing baseball. He is on a team. His team is called the Jays. Gabe is happy when his team wins.**

What is the name of Gabe's baseball team?

(A) the Cubs

(B) the Hawks

(C) the Jays

(D) the Reds

Write how you know.

_____

_____

5. **Ali went to the beach. She went with her mom and sister. Ali had fun playing at the beach.**

Which picture fits with the passage?

(A)

(B)

(C)

(D)

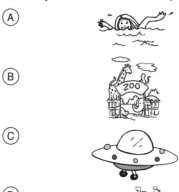

Write how you know.

_____

_____

6. **Maria and her mom went fishing. Maria's mom packed a picnic. It was a fun day. Maria could not wait to go home and tell her dad what she had done!**

Write how the picture adds information to the passage.

_____

_____

Name _____   Date _____

Compare and Contrast Two Texts
Reading: Literature and Informational Text

DIRECTIONS: Read the passages. Then, answer the questions using details from the passages.

Interesting Snakes

Snakes are interesting animals. Snakes live almost everywhere on Earth. Snakes live on land. Snakes live in water. Snakes do not live at the South Pole. Snakes can move without legs! They squeeze and stretch their muscles to slide across the land. Snakes do not have eyelids. They cannot blink. They cannot close their eyes to sleep. Snakes cannot see well. If you stand very still, a snake might not even notice you! Snakes are very interesting animals.

Dangerous Snakes

Snakes are very dangerous. Snakes can strike very fast. Some snakes eat small animals. They swallow them whole! Other snakes squeeze their prey. Other snakes have poison. They bite their prey. The poison can kill the prey. People must be careful in areas with snakes. If a snake is startled, it may bite you. Snakes are very dangerous animals.

Strategy   As you read, compare information that is the same and identify information that is different.

Test Tip   Reading two passages on the same topic can help you learn more about the topic.

1. **What is the main topic of the first passage?**

   (A) Snakes are interesting.

   (B) Snakes are dangerous.

   (C) Snakes live almost everywhere on Earth.

   (D) Snakes do not have eyelids.

   Write how you know.

   _____

   _____

2. **Write the main topic of the second passage.**

   _____

3. **What is the same about the two passages?**

   _____

   _____

4. **Which two details show what the author of the second passage thinks about snakes?**

   (A) "People must be careful in areas with snakes."

   (B) "Some snakes eat small animals."

   (C) "If a snake is startled, it may bite you."

   (D) "Snakes are very dangerous animals."

5. **How are the two passages different?**

   (A) The first passage tells facts about snakes. The second passage tells opinions.

   (B) The first author thinks snakes are interesting.The second author thinks snakes are dangerous.

   (C) The first passage is made up. The second passage is real.

   (D) The first author hates snakes. The second author loves snakes.

Name _____ Date _____

Compare Two Texts
Reading: Literature and Informational Text

DIRECTIONS: Read the passages. Then, answer the questions using details from the passages.

Frogs

Frogs can live in many different places. They can live on the side of a mountain. They can live in the hot desert. They can live in rain forests. Frogs can live on land. They can live in the water. They can even live in trees!

Toads

Toads are a lot like frogs. Toads live in many places that frogs live. But, toads only live on land. They cannot live in the water. They cannot live in trees. Toads look a lot like frogs. A toad's body is fatter than a frog's body. Toads have shorter back legs. Toads are slower than frogs.

Strategy Find reasons, or details, that tell how the author thinks about the topic. These reasons will help you find the main topic or main idea.

Test Tip Reread both passages to find all of the information.

1. **What is the main topic of the first passage?**

   (A) Frogs can live in many different places.

   (B) Frogs are interesting.

   (C) Frogs are nothing like toads.

   (D) Frogs can live in trees.

   Write how you know.

   _____

   _____

2. **Write the main topic of the second passage.**

   _____

   _____

3. **What new information is given in the second passage?**

   _____

   _____

Write how you know.

   _____

   _____

4. **Where can frogs live that toads cannot?**

   _____

   _____

5. **Which two key details in the passage "Toads" support the main idea?**

   (A) Frogs can live in water, but toads can't.

   (B) Frogs can live on the side of a mountain.

   (C) Frogs can even live in trees.

   (D) Frogs can live in trees, but toads can't.

6. **Which passage tells more about how frogs and toads are the same and different?**

   _____

   _____

Use Nouns and Verbs
Language

DIRECTIONS: Read the sentence and the word choices. Choose the best word or phrase to fill in the blank.

Strategy
Ask yourself what a noun names. Does it name a person, place, or thing?

Strategy
Identify words that name an action. Then, identify if the action is happening now, has already happened, or will happen in the future.

Test Tip
There are different kinds of nouns: common, proper, and possessive.

Test Tip
Possessive nouns have apostrophes and the letter s: Mary's.

Common nouns	Name a person, place, or thing: *cat, house, spoon*
Proper nouns	Name people or places: *Mike, Mrs. Jennings, The White House, Principal Green*
Possessive nouns	Show what belongs to a person, place, or thing: *Greta's bike, the park's playground*

Present verbs	Tells about an action that happened today: *I walk home. I cook dinner.*
Past verbs	Tells about an action that already happened: *I walked home yesterday. I cooked dinner on Monday.*
Future verbs	Tells about an action that will happened: *I will walk home tomorrow. I will cook dinner next week.*

1. _____ dog likes to run.

   (A) Cara

   (B) Cara's

   (C) Girl

   (D) Girls

   Write how you know.

   _____

   _____

2. _____ new bike is bright red.

   (A) Bill's

   (B) Bills

   (C) Bills's

   (D) Bill

3. That room belongs to my brother. It is my _____ room.

   _____

4. The boat sinks into the water.

   Which type of verb is used in this sentence, present, past, or future?

   _____

   Write how you know.

   _____

   _____

English Language Arts

Use Nouns and Verbs
Language

DIRECTIONS: Choose or write the correct answer.

Strategy Ask yourself how many nouns are in the sentence. Is only one person, place, or thing in the sentence? Is there more than one?

Test Tip Nouns that are singular name one person, place or thing. They go with verbs that end in –s: The cat plays.

Test Tip

Proper nouns start with a capital letter.

5. For each common noun, write a proper noun on the line.

dog   _____

girl   _____

teacher   _____

school   _____

6. A caterpillar _____ leaves.

(A) eating

(B) eated

(C) eat

(D) eats

Test Tip

Nouns that are plural name more than one person, place or thing. Verbs do not have an –s at the end: The cats play.

7. The boys _____ at the ice rink in winter.

(A) skates

(B) skated

(C) skate

(D) skater

8. Write a sentence using each noun and verb.

friend, meet

_____

_____

girls, walk

_____

_____

9. Write the word correctly on the line.

The cat belongs to Leesa.

It is _____ cat.

10. Write a sentence that tells an action that you will do in the future.

_____

_____

Use Pronouns
Language

DIRECTIONS: Choose or write the best answer.

Strategy — To identify pronouns, ask yourself *Who is doing the action?*

Test Tip — A pronoun stands in for a noun. Some pronouns include *I, me, my, they, them, their, anyone, everything.* Singular nouns use *he, she, it.* Plural nouns use *they, them.*

EXAMPLE

Which sentence uses the correct pronoun?

- (A) They gave the book to I.
- ● They gave the book to me.
- (C) They gave the book to she.
- (D) They gave the book to we.

1. **That rabbit belongs to Gina. Which sentence means the same thing?**
   - (A) That is her rabbit.
   - (B) That is she's rabbit.
   - (C) That is she rabbit.
   - (D) That is mine rabbit.

2. **Rewrite the sentence correctly on the line.**
   I am going to she's house to play.
   _____

3. **Write the pronoun that replaces the underlined noun in the sentence below.**
   Please give <u>the pencil</u> to me _____.

4. **Explain why this sentence is not correct. Write your answer on the lines.**
   My dad knows anything about cars.
   _____

5. **Rewrite the sentence and replace the underlined nouns with a pronoun.**
   <u>Matt and Pete</u> learned how to cook.
   _____

6. **Choose the sentence that uses a pronoun correctly.**
   - (A) We ate at them's restaurant.
   - (B) We ate at they's restaurant.
   - (C) We ate at our's restaurant.
   - (D) We ate at their restaurant.

7. **Rewrite the sentence with the correct pronoun.**
   That is mine favorite sweater.
   _____

8. **Rewrite the sentence and replace the underlined noun with a pronoun.**
   The students left to get <u>the students'</u> books.
   _____

English Language Arts

Use Pronouns
Language

DIRECTIONS: Choose or write the best answer.

Strategy | Identify the noun in a sentence to know if the pronoun is replacing one noun or more than one.

Test Tip | After using a pronoun, read the new sentence aloud to see if it sounds correct.

9. **Write a pronoun that correctly replaces the underlined noun.**

   <u>Beth and Tim</u> rode horses at the camp.

   _____

   Write how you know.

   _____

   _____

   _____

10. **Choose the correct pronoun for the underlined word.**

    I met <u>Tom</u> at school.

    Ⓐ she

    Ⓑ him

    Ⓒ her

    Ⓓ them

    Rewrite each sentence with the correct pronoun.

11. **She and me went to the park.**

    _____

12. **Us saw Angel and Chris there.**

    _____

13. **Which nouns replace the pronoun in this sentence?**

    They went down the slide.

    Ⓐ Marty

    Ⓑ Marty and Jason

    Ⓒ Lisa

    Ⓓ I

14. **Which pronoun replaces the underlined nouns in this sentence?**

    <u>Kate and Brad</u> flew a kite.

    Ⓐ Them

    Ⓑ Us

    Ⓒ We

    Ⓓ It

English Language Arts

Use Verb Tense
Language

DIRECTIONS: Choose or write the best answer.

> **Strategy**   Look at the endings of verbs to identify if the action is happening now, in the past, or in the future.

> **Test Tip**   Different endings show if an action happens *now*, in the *past*, or in the *future*.

Present verbs	No special ending: *I walk home. I cook dinner.*
Past verbs	Add *–ed* to the verb. *I walked home yesterday. I cooked dinner on Monday.*
Future verbs	Add the word *will* before the verb: *I will walk home tomorrow. I will cook dinner next week.*

1. **Read the sentences. Then, answer the questions.**

   Tomorrow we go to the zoo. I will see a zebra. The zebra will eat grass.

   Which verb correctly replaces *go* in the first sentence?

   (A) go

   (B) goed

   (C) gos

   (D) will go

   Write how you know.

   _____

   _____

   _____

2. **Which word should replace *I* in the second sentence before the verb?**

   (A) eats

   (B) we

   (C) is

   (D) I

3. **Write 3 sentences that use the present, past, and future. Use the verb *clean*.**

   _____

   _____

   _____

4. **Which verbs are past tense?**

   (A) smelling

   (B) dances

   (C) filled

   (D) waited

5. **Write the correct form of the underlined words on the line.**

   Rose <u>is grin</u> at the joke she heard.

   _____

> **Test Tip**
>
> Another way to form a present verb is to use the word *is* and the ending *–ing:*
> He is dancing.

Name _____   Date _____

Use Verb Tense
Language

DIRECTIONS: Choose or write the best answer.

Strategy | Find clue words that tell if an action happens in the past or future— *have, had, will.*

Test Tip | Use each verb in a sentence to help you choose the correct answer. For example: I wait. I waited. I will wait.

EXAMPLE

Complete the chart. Use present, past, and future verbs.

Present	Past	Future
works	worked	will work
paints	painted	will paint

6. **Complete the chart. Use present, past, and future verbs.**

Present	Past	Future
		will jump
		will smile

7. **Which of these sentences is correct? Choose two.**

(A) Add *–ed* to most past verbs: They talked.

(B) Use the word *is* and *are* to form future verbs.

(C) Do not add an *–s* to verbs with plural nouns: They stop.

(D) All present verbs have singular nouns.

8. **Write the sentence below using the correct verbs. Mara and Pam plays the piano tomorrow.**

_____

_____

9. **What type of verb tells about an action that is happening now?**

_____

10. **Choose two answers that list correct present, past, future verbs.**

(A) chase, chases, will chase

(B) add, added, will add

(C) handing, hands, is hand

(D) mover, moving, moved.

Use Adjectives
Language

DIRECTIONS: Choose or write the correct answer.

Strategy Find adjectives that tell about how a noun looks or acts. Then, ask yourself what the adjective is describing.

EXAMPLE

Choose two answers that make sense in the sentence.

Paul climbed a _____ tree.

● tall

Ⓑ yellow

Ⓒ bad

● big

What did the words tell you about the tree?

Possible Answer: The size of the tree.

1. **What groups of adjectives tell about the sounds a puppy makes?**

Ⓐ loud, quiet, squeaky

Ⓑ brown, black, white

Ⓒ small, big, tall

Ⓓ soft, furry, fluffy

2. **The _____ boy smiled. Choose two words that tell about the boy.**

Ⓐ angry

Ⓑ nice

Ⓒ sad

Ⓓ happy

3. **Which words tell how many toys you might have?**

Ⓐ yellow, blue

Ⓑ two, three

Ⓒ little, small

Ⓓ quiet, loud

Write how you know.

_____

_____

4. **Complete the chart with the words that go together.**

Words: happy, large, red, tiny, tall, sad, yellow

Size	Color	Feelings
	blue	
big		excited

Write how the words in the last column are alike.

_____

_____

6. **Write three words that tell about ice cream flavors.**

_____

_____

English Language Arts

Use Adjectives
Language

DIRECTIONS: Choose or write the correct answer.

> **Strategy**
>
> Sort adjectives into categories, or groups, to help you understand words. For example, group all the words that tell about a noun's size, such as *big, large, huge, small, tiny,* or *little*.

7. **Which category, or group, would describe the places below?**

   library, school, reading room

   (A) places with books

   (B) people who read

   (C) things with words

   (D) places with animals

   Write how you know.

   _____

   _____

8. **What kinds of nouns might you find in a category called People In a Hospital? Write three words.**

   _____

   _____

9. **Choose two lists of words that tell about farms.**

   (A) trucks, cars, bikes

   (B) teacher, student, principal

   (C) barn, pen, house

   (D) cows, horses, hens

> **Test Tip**
>
> Riddles use adjectives to describe, or tell about, a noun.

EXAMPLE

Read the riddle. Write the answer on the line.

I am big.

I am red.

I go to fires.

What am I? _fire truck_

10. **Write a riddle that describes the sun.**

    I am _____.

    I am _____.

    I am _____.

    What am I? _____

11. **Write a riddle that describes a mouse.**

    I am _____.

    I sound _____.

    I eat _____.

    What am I? _____

12. **Adjectives tell about _____.**

Name _____ Date _____

Use Articles and Prepositions
Language

DIRECTIONS: Choose or write the correct answer.

Strategy
Identify prepositions by asking where a person, place, or thing is in a sentence. Or, find words that tell about time or when an action happens.

Test Tip
Some words tell where a person, place, or thing is, such as The glass is *on* the table or We sit *in* our chairs. Other words tell about time, such as We did not talk *during* class or I saw the movie *on* Monday. Words that tell where or when are prepositions. Read each sentence and make sure the preposition makes sense. For example, a glass can sit *on* a table, not *over* or *above* a table.

1. **The spider sits _____ the web.**
   - (A) above
   - (B) over
   - (C) on
   - (D) after

   Write how you know.

   _____

   _____

2. **Three apples are _____ the tree.**

Strategy
Ask yourself if the nouns name a specific, or exact noun (the), or if they name any noun (a/an).

Test Tip
An article is like an adjective because it tells about nouns. The word *a* tells if a noun is any person, place, or noun, like *a school*. The words *the* and *this* tells if a noun is about a specific, or exact, person, place or thing, like *the school* or *this school*.

EXAMPLES
   We read _a_ book in class every day.

Test Tip
Look for clues in the sentence. The answer is *a*. You would not read the same book every day.

   We read _the_ book today in class.

Test Tip
Look for clues in the sentence. The answer is *the*. The sentence tells about a specific, or exact, book.

3. **My mom picked _____ blue flowers this morning.**
   - (A) a
   - (B) the
   - (C) on
   - (D) in

   Write how you know.

   _____

   _____

English Language Arts

Use Articles and Prepositions
Language

DIRECTIONS: Choose or write the correct answer.

Strategy | Make a list of prepositions that tell where (*on, under, over, above, in*) and prepositions that tell when (*during, before, after*). Use your list to find the best prepositions to use in a sentence.

Test Tip | Remember that prepositions can also tell about time. Some prepositions tell where *and* when, such as *on* and *at*: The book is *on* the shelf. The play is *on* Tuesday. We see the bird *at* the park. Lunch is *at* noon.

4. We are going to see _____ movie everyone is talking about.

   (A) a
   (B) into
   (C) the
   (D) above

5. I saw blue birds _____

   a tree branch _____ Monday.

6. **Complete each sentence with a preposition.**

   Yesterday I went for _____ bike ride.

   I rode _____ the park.

   I rode _____ the bridge.

Test Tip

To tell about a specific noun, use the word *the*, like *I see the door to my classroom.* You can also use the words *this* and *that* for singular nouns. Use *these* or *those* for plural nouns.

7. **Which words complete the sentence below?**

   I saw _____ shoes we need for basketball

   _____ the store.

   (A) a, over
   (B) these, at
   (C) this, on
   (D) that, into

Test Tip

For words that begin with a vowel sound, use the article *an*: I ate an apple.

8. **Which article is correct in the sentence below?**
   Dad made [a/an] egg for breakfast.

   _____

9. **Which word is incorrect in the sentence below?**
   We saw a elephant at the zoo.
   Write the sentence so it is correct.

   _____

   _____

Name _____ Date _____

Use Capitals and Punctuation
Language

DIRECTIONS: Read the sentences. Choose or write the correct punctuation mark.

Strategy | Read each sentence aloud to yourself to help you decide which punctuation mark is needed.

Test Tip | Most sentences have periods at the end. Sentences with a lot of feeling have exclamation points. Sentences that ask a question get a question mark.

EXAMPLES

The horse ran

- (A) ?
- ● .
- (C) !
- (D) ,

How old are you ____?____

1. I like peanut butter
   - (A) .
   - (B) ?
   - (C) !
   - (D) ,

2. May Tish come over _____

   Write how you know.

   _____

   _____

3. That butterfly is so pretty _____

   Write how you know.

   _____

   _____

4. Harvey caught a fish _____

5. I will eat lunch _____

6. Write a sentence that uses an exclamation point (!) at the end.

   _____

   _____

7. I walked to the library _____

   Write how you know.

   _____

   _____

   _____

8. Write a question that uses a question mark (?) at the end.

   _____

   _____

English Language Arts

Use Capitals and Punctuation
Language

DIRECTIONS: Read the sentences. Choose or write the best answer.

Strategy | Learn the rules of capitalization and try to remember them as you read and write.

Test Tip | All sentences begin with capital letters. Names and place names begin with a capital letter. Ask yourself if a noun is a person's name, a place, or a month in a date. These nouns are capitalized.

EXAMPLE

Choose the word that should be capitalized.

We got a new dog. We named her cotton candy. She is gold and brown.

(A) Dog

● Cotton Candy

(C) Gold

(D) Brown

Choose or write the word that should be capitalized.

9. **Jack played with tommy today.**

_____

10. **Mr. Sanders bought a new puppy on monday.**

(A) mr.

(B) Bought

(C) Puppy

(D) Monday

11. **We ran in a race. It was on Saturday. jacob won!**

_____

12. **Sue and Stacy are twins. Their birthday is on december 22.**

_____

Test Tip

Commas show a pause, or a short stop. Commas are used if there are three or more things listed: *We have a cat, a dog, and a bird.* Dates have commas after the day: *June 1, 2015.*

13. **Choose the sentence that is written correctly.**

(A) I ran in a race on saturday, april 10 2014

(B) I ran in a race on Saturday, April 10, 2014.

(C) I ran in a Race on Saturday April 10, 2014?

(D) I ran in a race on saturday, april 10 201 4.

14. **Write why the sentence is not correct.**

My parrot is green yellow and red.

_____

_____

_____

15. **Rewrite the sentence correctly on the line.**

do you know mark hailey or megan

_____

_____

Name _____ Date _____

English Language Arts

Understand Types of Sentences
Language

DIRECTIONS: Choose or write the correct answer.

Strategy — Ask yourself if a sentence has a noun and a verb. If it does, it is a complete sentence.

Test Tip — Ask yourself what is missing from the sentence, a noun (a person, place, or thing) or a verb (a word that tells about an action).

1. Choose the complete sentence.

  (A) The butterfly.

  (B) Moon beam.

  (C) The sun sets.

  (D) Ran home.

Write how you know.

_____

_____

Test Tip

Don't forget that complete sentences have punctuation at the end.

2. Which two choices can you put together to make a complete sentence?

  (A) by the pond

  (B) A frog hopped

  (C) furry kitten

  (D) He and his brother

Test Tip

Don't forget that complete sentences have punctuation at the end.

Write the complete sentence.

_____

3. What can you add to make the words below a complete sentence?

flew the kite

_____

_____

Write a complete sentence using the words.

_____

_____

4. Add a verb to the words to make it a complete sentence. Write it on the line.

bird nests in the tree

_____

5. Use the words to write a complete sentence.

Words:

Joe, Eva

park, tree

go, played

to, the, and, a

_____

_____

_____

_____

English Language Arts

Understand Types of Sentences
Language

DIRECTIONS: Choose or write the correct answer.

Strategy	Categorize sentences as sentences that tell something or tell someone to do something (end with a period), ask something (end with a question mark), or show a lot of feeling (end with an exclamation point).
Test Tip	Sentences can tell about something, ask a question, or tell someone to do something. Different types of sentences make stories more interesting. Look at the punctuation at the end to find out what kind of sentence it is. Sentences can also be joined together using the words *and, but, or,* and *because*.

EXAMPLES

Maria went to the store.

Did Juan see that movie?

Go home after school.

Ethan fed the dogs. They were hungry.

Ethan fed the dogs because they were hungry.

6. Join these sentences together. Write the new sentence on the line.

Ira ate a sandwich. He was hungry.

_____

_____

7. Do you want to go to the beach? Do you want to go to the pool?

What kind of sentences are these? _____

Write how you know.

_____

_____

Join these sentences together. Write the new sentence.

_____

_____

8. Choose two sentences that tell someone to do something.

Ⓐ Study for the spelling test.

Ⓑ We met at the library.

Ⓒ I love that story.

Ⓓ Sing me a song.

9. Join these sentences together. Write the new sentence.

Sue is sick. Jack gave her his cold.

_____

_____

10. Read that book. Tell me about it.

What kind of sentences are these? _____

Write how you know.

_____

_____

English Language Arts

Determine Word Meaning
Language

DIRECTIONS: Read the story. For each underlined word, find the best meaning.

Strategy   Read carefully to identify words in sentences that are clues to finding the meaning of unknown words.

Test Tip   Some words have more than one meaning. You can use other words in the sentence to find the meaning.

Aidan's Walk

Aidan took a walk around town with his parents. They decided to <u>head</u> to the library. Aidan picked out a book about baseball.

At the fire station, a truck flashed its <u>light</u>. The bright flashes hurt Aidan's <u>head</u>. Aidan stopped to talk to firefighter Tom. Tom used to play baseball when he was little.

Aidan saw his neighbor, Mrs. Loo, carrying a bag. The bag did not look <u>light</u>, so Aidan helped her carry it into her house. As he placed the bag next to the kitchen <u>sink</u>, Aidan talked to Mrs. Loo about his book.

Aidan and his parents went home. Aidan could not wait to <u>sink</u> into his book.

1. **Which meaning fits the sentence?**

   They decided to <u>head</u> to the library.

   (A) the part of the body that holds the brain

   (B) walk toward; walk to

   Write how you know.

   _____

   _____

2. **Choose two words in this sentence that help you find the meaning for <u>head</u>.**

   The bright flashes hurt Aidan's <u>head</u>.

   (A) hurt

   (B) bright

   (C) flashes

   (D) Aidan's

3. **Write the sentence from the story that uses the word *light* to mean "not heavy."**

   _____

   _____

4. **What is another way to say "The bag did not look <u>light</u>"?**

   (A) The bag was light.

   (B) The bag was empty.

   (C) The bag was not there.

   (D) The bag was heavy.

5. **Write the meaning of the word *sink* in the sentence from the story below.**

   Aidan could not wait to <u>sink</u> into his book.

   _____

   _____

English Language Arts

Determine Word Meaning
Language

DIRECTIONS: Choose or write the correct answer.

> ## Strategy
> Divide words into parts: prefix, root word, and suffix. Then, find the meaning of each part to understand the word.

> ## Test Tip
> Word parts can be added to the beginning or to the ending of words. If the word part *un-* means "not," you can find out that the word *untie* means "not tied."

EXAMPLE

Which word matches the meaning below?

"to play again"

- ● replay
- Ⓑ unplay
- Ⓒ played
- Ⓓ play's

6. **Use the words in the sentence and the word parts to find the meaning of the word unable.**

   We are unable to go to the party because we are sick.

   Meaning: _____

   Write how you know.

   _____

   _____

   Write the words from the sentence that helped you find the meaning of the word unable.

   _____

   _____

   How did these words help you?

   _____

   _____

> ## Test Tip
> The ending –er can mean "one who does." You can find out that the word baker means "one who bakes."

7. **Which word tells about a person who teaches?**
   - Ⓐ teaches
   - Ⓑ teacher
   - Ⓒ teach's
   - Ⓓ teaching

8. **Complete the chart with words that match the meanings.**

Word	Meaning
	one who writes
	not kind
	cover again

9. **Write the words below using the ending –er.**

   sing   clean   help   walk

   _____

English Language Arts

Write an Opinion
Writing

DIRECTIONS: An opinion paragraph tells how you feel about a topic. It gives reasons why you feel that way. Write an opinion paragraph for the school newspaper about your favorite season.

Your paragraph should have:

- A sentence that tells what your topic is.
- A sentence that tells how you feel about the topic.
- Some reasons for why you feel the way that you do.
- A sentence to end your paragraph.

Read the example paragraph to see how one student wrote an opinion paragraph about his favorite pet.

EXAMPLE

My favorite pet is a dog. I think dogs make the best pets. Dogs are friendly. They like to be close to you. They will wag their tail. Dogs protect you. They will bark if somebody comes to the house. I think dogs are the best pets.

Strategy
Use words such as *I think* or *I feel* to share your opinion Then, make sure you give reasons that tell why you think or feel the way you do.

Test Tip
Reread your paragraph. Did you use complete sentences? Did you capitalize dates and names of people? Did you use punctuation at the end of sentences?

_____

_____

_____

_____

_____

_____

_____

_____

English Language Arts

Write an Opinion
Writing

DIRECTIONS: An opinion paragraph tells how you feel about a topic. It gives reasons why you feel that way. Write an opinion paragraph for a class book about your favorite food.

Your paragraph should have:

- A sentence that tells what your topic is.
- A sentence that tells how you feel about the topic.
- Some reasons for why you feel the way that you do.
- A sentence to end your paragraph.

Read the example paragraph to see how one student wrote an opinion paragraph about her favorite holiday.

EXAMPLE

    My favorite holiday is Halloween. Halloween is on October 31 every year. I think Halloween is the most fun holiday of all. I like to get dressed up on Halloween. My favorite costume is a princess. I also like to go trick–or–treating on Halloween. I think it is fun to see everyone in their costumes. I think Halloween is the best holiday.

Test Tip   Reread your paragraph. Are all of your sentences about your favorite food? Make sure you focus only on the topic.

_____

_____

_____

_____

_____

_____

_____

_____

_____

_____

English Language Arts

Write an Informative Paragraph
Writing

DIRECTIONS: An informative paragraph gives facts about a topic. Use what you already know and the facts below to write an informative paragraph about healthy foods.

Your paragraph should have:

- A topic sentence
- Some facts about the topic
- A sentence to end your paragraph

Facts About Healthy Foods

Vegetables	Help you grow
Fruits	Keep you healthy
Whole grains	Keep bones strong
Nuts	Keep heart healthy
Water	Give you energy
Low sugar	Put you in a good mood
Low fat	Help your memory
Low salt	Help your brain work better

Strategy — Put a mark next to the facts you want to use in your paragraph.

Test Tip — Read your paragraph. Make sure it gives information—facts about the healthy food—and does not just list healthy foods.

_____

_____

_____

_____

_____

_____

_____

_____

_____

English Language Arts

Write an Explanatory Paragraph
Writing

DIRECTIONS: An explanatory paragraph gives directions for doing something. Choose a topic from the list. Write an explanatory paragraph telling how to do it.

Your paragraph should have:

- A topic sentence
- Clear steps to follow
- A sentence to end your paragraph

Topics	
How to make a sandwich (you pick what kind!)	How to play a game (you pick the game!)
How to make a bed	How to walk to school
How to wash a dog	How to brush your teeth

Strategy   After you choose a topic, make a list of the steps. Number the steps to keep track of what comes first, next, and last.

Test Tip   Use words like *first, next, then,* and *finally* to show the order of steps to follow.

_____

_____

_____

_____

_____

_____

_____

_____

_____

_____

_____

Write a Narrative
Writing

DIRECTIONS: A narrative is a story that describes an event. A narrative has lots of details. The details describe the events, or what happened. A narrative paints a picture in the mind of the reader. Write a narrative that answers the question, *Where is your favorite place to be?*

Your narrative should have:

- Two or more things that you do in that place
- Interesting details about what your place looks like
- Interesting details about what you do there
- Time words like *first, next, then,* and *finally*
- Adjectives to describe people, things, and events
- An ending sentence

Strategy   It helps to organize your details in a web. Organizing details helps you know which details are important to use and which ones you can skip.

Use the Graphic Organizer to plan your narrative. Write the name of your favorite place in the center circle. Write details about the place in the outer circles. Describe what you saw. Describe how you felt. Describe what you heard or smelled. Describe what you do in your favorite place. Add circles if you need more.

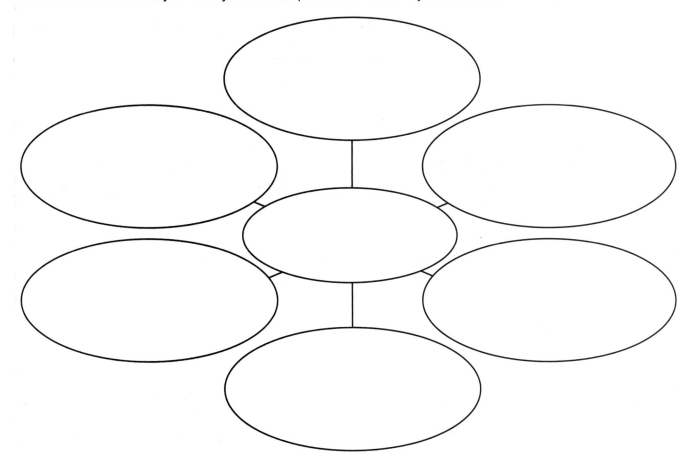

English Language Arts

Write a Narrative
Writing

> **Test Tip**
>
> Look back at your graphic organizer and reread all of the details about your favorite place. Which details are the most important? Use these details in your narrative. Before writing, read the directions one more time to make sure you include everything.

_____

_____

_____

_____

_____

_____

_____

_____

_____

_____

_____

_____

_____

_____

_____

_____

_____

_____

_____

English Language Arts

Strategy Review

In this section, you will review the strategies you learned and apply them to practice the skills.

Strategy Use details in the story to make a picture in your mind as you read. Use details to show your understanding.

When you read a story, think about the details as you read. Make connections to things you already know about a topic. Make connections to another story you read. Use these details and connections to help you understand the story better.

Read the story carefully. Then, answer the questions using details from the story.

> Mr. Weinstein took his children to the zoo. Austin wanted to see the flamingoes. He liked how they stood on one leg. Ethan wanted to see the giraffes. Giraffes were Ethan's favorite animal. Mr. Weinstein wanted to see the bears. He liked how they played together.

First, read the story. Think about what you know about zoos.

Next, make a connection. When you go to a zoo, what animals do you like to visit? Why do you like to visit that animal? Compare characters to make more connections. How are they alike? How are they different?

Finally, read the questions that go with the story. Reread the story if you need to. Look for key words in the question and then, find the answers in the story.

1. **What animal did Austin want to visit?**
   (A) giraffe
   (B) lion
   (C) bear
   (D) flamingo

> Next, he visited the giraffes. Their long necks reached into the treetops. They were having a tasty breakfast of oak leaves. Finally, the zookeeper went by the bear habitat. The baby bears were rolling around together in the dirt. They looked like they were having a great time.

2. **Why did Mr. Weinstein want to go see the bears?**
   (A) He liked how they stood on one leg.
   (B) He liked how they played together.
   (C) They were his favorite animal.
   (D) He liked to watch them eat.

Read the next story about a zoo. Think about how it is the same as the story you just read. Think about how it is different.

> It was a bright, warm morning. The zookeeper was making his rounds. First, he stopped to see the flamingoes. He watched them clean their pink feathers. He gave them some shrimp for breakfast.

3. **What words helped you make a picture in your mind?**

_____

_____

_____

4. **Write how the two stories are alike.**

_____

_____

English Language Arts

Strategy Review

Strategy   Look carefully at pictures to help you understand words better.

The White Spaceship
One night I was in the woods. I saw a bright, white spaceship. It was sitting under some trees. I was scared, but I tried to be brave. I was afraid the aliens might take me away to their planet. Suddenly, the spaceship opened. A girl stepped out. She had green skin and three eyes!

First, read the story and make connections to the details. Who is in the story? Where does the story take place? What can you picture in your mind?

Next, study the picture. Ask yourself how the picture adds details that are not in the story. Then, use the picture and details from the story to help you answer the questions.

1. Write what the spaceship looked like.

_____

_____

2. How did the character feel when they saw the spaceship?

(A) excited

(B) afraid

(C) happy

(D) sad

3. How did the strategy help you answer these questions?

_____

_____

Read the story carefully. Then, answer the questions.

The Candy Bar
One day Mom went to the store. She bought food for dinner. She also bought a treat for each of her children. She bought Jennifer a chocolate candy bar. She bought Paul a peanut butter candy bar.

Mom got home from the store. She gave Paul the two candy bars.

"You can eat one, but put Jennifer's candy bar in the refrigerator, please," she told Paul.

A little while later, Paul came into the kitchen. Mom was chopping vegetables for dinner. He went to the refrigerator. He took out a candy bar and started eating it. Mom looked at the chocolate around Paul's mouth.

"That's your sister's candy bar," she said.

"No, it's not," said Paul. "I already ate hers. This one's mine."

4. What was the problem in the story?

(A) Mom bought one candy bar for two children.

(B) Paul ate Jennifer's candy bar.

(C) Jennifer ate Paul's candy bar.

(D) Mom didn't buy any treats for her kids.

5. Paul knew he was not supposed to eat the second candy bar. How do you think Mom will react?

_____

_____

English Language Arts

Strategy Review

Strategy   Plan your writing using a graphic organizer.

Julio wanted to write a paragraph that tells how pigs and ducks are different and alike. He started by planning his paragraph. He used a graphic organizer called a Venn diagram to organize the information he wanted to include.

First, Julio wrote information that is true about pigs, but not about ducks.

Pigs   **Both**   **Ducks**
Play in mud
Have curly tails
Have live babies

Next, Julio wrote information that is true about ducks, but not pigs.

Pigs   **Both**   **Ducks**
Play in mud   Quack
Have curly tails   Lay eggs
Have live babies   Swim in water

Finally, Julio wrote information that is true about both ducks and pigs.

Pigs   **Both**   **Ducks**
Play in mud   Animals   Quack
Have curly tails Live on farms Lay eggs
Have live babies   Swim in water

Use the graphic organizer to collect details about pets.

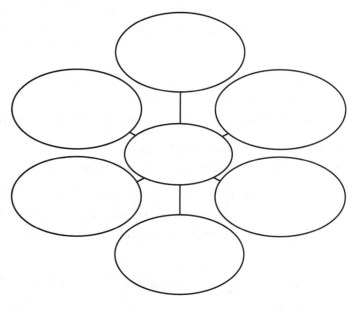

Write a paragraph about pets.

_____

_____

_____

_____

_____

_____

_____

_____

_____

_____

English Language Arts

Strategy Review

Strategy Revise to make sure your writing is clear and makes sense. Then, edit to fix errors.

After you write your first draft, you should reread it. Read the story aloud to yourself to make sure it makes sense. Look for places where the reader might have trouble understanding what you want to say. Look for words that need capitals. Look for places that need punctuation marks. Finally, look for words that might be spelled wrong.

> Once upon a time, there was a little girl name hannah. She lived with her mother and father in the woods she was very nice. All of the animals played with her. They went to the village one day. They bought a cake. Then, they went home and had a party.

First, read the story to make sure it makes sense.
There is a sentence that is not very clear: "They went to the village one day." Does this mean the family or the animals? Rewrite the sentence to make it clear. "Hannah and her parents went to the village one day."

Next, look for words that need capitals.
Hannah is a name, so it should have a capital letter.

Then, look for places that need punctuation marks.
There is a run–on sentence: "She lived with her mother and father in the woods she was very nice."
Put a period after woods. Use a capital letter for she.

Finally, look for spelling mistakes.
"Once upon a time, there was a little girl name Hannah." There should be a d at the end of *name***.**

1. **Find the mistakes in this sentence. Then, write the sentence correctly on the lines.**

James and marta went shoping at the mall?

_____

_____

2. **Find the mistakes in this sentence. Then, write the sentence correctly on the lines.**

Do you like chocolate or vanilla? Chocolates my favrit.

_____

_____

Strategies for Mathematics Tests

Read the strategies below to learn more about how they work.

Use basic operations to solve problems.

You can use what you know about adding, subtracting, multiplying, and dividing to solve many different types of problems. Make sure you know your basic math facts. This will save time on the test and make sure your answers are correct.

Use graphs, tables, and drawings to understand data.

Sometimes, making a drawing of a word problem helps you figure out how to solve it. Other times, making a graph or line plot is a way to show numbers or amounts of something. Drawings, number lines, line plots, and other graphs all use numbers.

Read word problems carefully. Make sure you know what you are asked to do.

Whenever you need to solve a word problem, you should first ask *What information do I know?* Then, you should ask *What question am I being asked to answer?* or *What am I being asked to find?* Don't start solving until you know the answers to these questions.

Choose the right tools and units to measure objects.

Certain tools are used to measure length, weight, and temperature. Remember that measurements all have units. Lengths are often measured in inches (in.), feet (ft.), centimeters (cm), or meters (m). Weight is often measured in pounds (lb.), grams (g), or kilograms (kg). Temperature can be measured in degrees Celsius (°C) or degrees Fahrenheit (°F).

Use what you know about numbers, shapes, and measurement to answer questions.

Using what you already know about numbers, shapes, and measurement, you can answer many different types of questions.

Solve Problems: Add Within 20
Operations and Algebraic Thinking

DIRECTIONS: Read the problems. Then, answer the questions.

EXAMPLE

Mia has 6 apples. She buys 2 more apples. Write numbers to complete the number sentence to find out how many apples Mia has all together.

_____ ☐ _____ = _____

6 + 2 = 8

Mia has 8 apples all together.

Strategy When using addition, ask yourself what you are adding and how many of each.

Test Tip Read carefully to understand what the problem asks you to do. Problems may ask you to put together numbers, add numbers, or compare numbers.

1. Kim and Lisa counted birds. Kim counted 5 birds and Lisa counted 8 birds. Write a number sentence that shows how many birds they counted in all.

   _____

2. Carlos bought a notebook at the school store for 10¢. He also bought a pencil for 5¢. How much did Carlos spend in all? Use words, numbers, or pictures to show how you found your answer.

3. David read 9 pages in his book on Monday. On Tuesday, he read 2 more pages than he did on Monday. How many pages did David read on Tuesday?

   _____

Write a sentence that tells how you found your answer.

_____

_____

_____

_____

4. Six horses were eating grass in a field. More horses ran into the field. Now there are 14 horses in the field. Which number sentence shows how many horses ran into the field?

   (A) 6 + 8 = 14
   (B) 14 + 6 = 20
   (C) 6 + 6 = 12
   (D) 7 + 7 = 14

Write how you found the answer.

_____

_____

Solve Problems: Add Within 20
Operations and Algebraic Thinking

Strategy   Find clue words that tell you that you need to add, such as *how many*, 8 *more*, and *in all*.

5. Luke has 6 marbles. Mark has 12 marbles. Which number sentence shows how many marbles they have in all?

   (A) $12 - 6 = 6$

   (B) $6 - 6 = 0$

   (C) $12 + 4 = 16$

   (D) $12 + 6 = 18$

6. Write a number sentence that can be used to find how many shapes are in this group in all. Explain how you found your answer.

_____

_____

_____

Test Tip

Look at the operation sign in the number sentence. This will tell you if you need to write a problem that asks for a sum (add) or a difference (subtract).

7. Write a story problem that can be solved using this number sentence.

$$5 + 6 = 11$$

_____

_____

_____

_____

8. Milo had 9 ribbons. He ran a race and won 1 more ribbon. Milo says he now has 19 ribbons. Is he correct? Tell how you know.

_____

_____

_____

_____

9. Complete the number sentence by writing the missing number in the box.

$$13 + \boxed{} = 18$$

10. Which number pairs make this number sentence true? Choose all that are correct.

$$\boxed{} + \boxed{} = 16$$

   (A) 5 and 10

   (B) 7 and 9

   (C) 10 and 6

   (D) 5 and 11

   (E) 8 and 8

   (F) 4 and 13

11. Last week, Ray invited 12 people to his picnic. This week, he invited 8 more people. Write a number sentence to show how many people he invited.

_____

Solve Problems: Subtract Within 20
Operations and Algebraic Thinking

DIRECTIONS: Choose the best answer.

Strategy Show your answer in different ways: drawings, number sentences, and word problems.

Test Tip Draw objects to help you write a number sentence.

EXAMPLE:

There were 5 books. Two fell off the table. Which number sentence shows how many were left?

Ⓐ 3 − 1 = 2
● 5 − 2 = 3
Ⓒ 3 − 2 = 1
Ⓓ 4 − 2 = 2

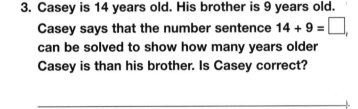

1. Rosa's mom baked 9 large cookies. She gave 2 to Rosa. Write a number sentence that you can use to find how many cookies Rosa's mom has left.

The ☐ stands for the number of cookies that Rosa's mom has left.

_____ − _____ = ☐

2. Solve your number sentence to tell how many cookies Rosa's mom has left.

_____

_____

Test Tip

Words like *how much farther* and *how many were left* usually mean you will need to subtract.

3. Casey is 14 years old. His brother is 9 years old. Casey says that the number sentence 14 + 9 = ☐ can be solved to show how many years older Casey is than his brother. Is Casey correct?

_____

4. Write how you know how many years older Casey is than his brother.

_____

_____

_____

_____

_____

5. Alexi times how many seconds it takes her to run to the end of her driveway. Her fastest time is the difference of 19 − 6. Choose all of the number sentences that show a time that is less than Alexi's time.

Ⓐ 16 − 8 = ☐
Ⓑ 14 − 2 = ☐
Ⓒ 18 − 9 = ☐
Ⓓ 15 − 1 = ☐

Solve Problems: Subtract Within 20
Operations and Algebraic Thinking

6. Kyle read his book for 15 minutes. Kevin read his book for 10 minutes. Aram read his book for 14 minutes. Felipe read his book for 9 minutes. Who read his book for 17 minutes – 3 minutes? Tell how you know.

_____

_____

7. Jake has 15 car stickers. He gave his friend 9 of the stickers. How many car stickers does Jake have now? Draw a picture and write a number sentence to show how you found your answer.

8. Lia gave her friends some fruit juice and had 3 glasses left. How many glasses of fruit juice did Lia give to her friends? Use numbers or pictures to show your work.

9. Hana has 20 pieces of fruit that are pears and apples. Nine of them are apples. Use words, numbers, or pictures to find how many pears she has.

10. Each student is growing one tomato plant for the school garden. Dario's plant is 8 inches tall. Tula's plant is 13 inches tall. How much taller is Tula's plant than Dario's?

_____

11. Tell how you found your answer. Use words, numbers, or pictures.

12. Which number sentence has a difference of 6? Choose all that apply.

Ⓐ 12 – 6 = ☐
Ⓑ 15 – 8 = ☐
Ⓒ 13 – 7 = ☐
Ⓓ 16 – 4 = ☐

13. Write a subtraction story problem for the picture below.

_____

_____

14. Write a subtraction number sentence for your problem. Use a box for the difference.

_____

15. Solve your number sentence.

Solve Problems: Add 3 Whole Numbers

Operations and Algebraic Thinking

DIRECTIONS: Answer the questions.

Strategy Add three numbers in different ways. Add the numbers in order. Or make a ten first and then, add the other number.

EXAMPLE

Liza has some fruit. She has 3 apples, 4 pears, and 6 oranges.

Write a number sentence you can use to find how many pieces of fruit Liza has in all. The ☐ represents the unknown number.

_3_ + _4_ + _6_ = ☐ pieces of fruit

Show one way to add the three numbers and tell how many pieces of fruit Liza has in all.

I can add 4 plus 6 and get 10, and add on 3 more to make 13. Liza has 13 pieces of fruit.

1. Jake scored 3 goals, Trey scored 5 goals, and Pedro scored 7 goals. How many goals did the boys score in all?

   Ⓐ 8
   Ⓑ 10
   Ⓒ 12
   Ⓓ 15

2. Choose the number sentences that have a sum of 18.

   Ⓐ 6 + 3 + 8 = ☐
   Ⓑ 7 + 8 + 3 = ☐
   Ⓒ 9 + 6 + 3 = ☐
   Ⓓ 8 + 2 + 8 = ☐

3. Write an addition number sentence for the picture below. Use a ☐ for the total number of birds.

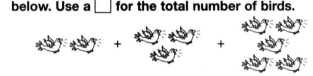

_____

4. Complete your number sentence to tell how many birds in all.

_____

5. 10 + 5 is the same as _____.

   Ⓐ 4 + 7 + 6
   Ⓑ 6 + 2 + 8
   Ⓒ 3 + 3 + 7
   Ⓓ 5 + 5 + 5

6. Mrs. Cruz ran 4 miles yesterday and 2 miles today. She will run 4 miles tomorrow. How many miles will Mrs. Cruz run in all? Use numbers and a picture to show how you know.

Solve Problems: Add 3 Whole Numbers
Operations and Algebraic Thinking

Strategy When writing number sentences, first, write the numbers you have from the problem. Then, write the operation sign needed. Finally, solve for the missing number.

7. Alonzo raked 3 + 6 + 7 bags of leaves. Rachel raked the same number of bags of leaves as Alonzo. Which two number sentences show the number of bags of leaves that Rachel raked in all?

Ⓐ ☐ = 5 + 5 + 3

Ⓑ ☐ = 3 + 10 + 3

Ⓒ ☐ = 9 + 7 + 0

Ⓓ ☐ = 7 + 5 + 3

8. Rita drew the picture below.

Write an addition number sentence that can be used to find the number of circles, squares, and stars in all. Use a ☐ for the number of shapes in all.

_____ + _____ + _____ = ☐ shapes

9. Solve your number sentence and tell how many shapes there are in all.

_____

_____

Test Tip Another way to add three numbers is to add the doubles first and then, add on the other number.

10. Tell two ways to find 7 + 3 + 3.

_____

_____

_____

_____

11. Jana made the number puzzle below for her friends to solve. Add across and down to find the sums. Write the sums in the boxes.

7	0	2	☐
2	7	6	☐
5	5	4	☐
☐	☐	☐	

Math

Use Properties of Operations: Add

Operations and Algebraic Thinking

DIRECTIONS: Answer the questions.

Strategy | Write addition problems in a different order to find the sum and check your answer: 3 + 9 = 12, 9 + 3 = 12, 12 = 9 + 3.

Test Tip | If you add numbers together in any order, you will get the same sum.

EXAMPLE:

The number sentence 2 + 3 = 5 is represented by the picture below.

Write another number sentence by changing the order of the first two numbers. Find the sum.

So, 2 birds plus 3 birds is the same as 3 birds plus 2 birds. The sum is 5 birds.

1. Choose two number sentences that are the same as 8 + 11.

   (A) 19 + 1

   (B) 11 + 8

   (C) 12 + 7

   (D) 11 + 5

2. Without adding, tell how you know, that the sum of 6 + 5 is the same as the sum of 5 + 6. Use words, numbers, or pictures.

3. Janis has 8 colors of paint. Mrs. Song gives her 7 more colors. Write two number sentences to show how many colors of paint Janis has now.

   _____

   _____

Test Tip

Changing the order or grouping of 3 or more numbers when you add does not change the sum.

4. Three friends find shells at the beach. Ali finds 4 shells. Lina finds 6 shells. Clara finds 2 shells. Each girl wrote a different number sentence to find how many shells they found in all.

   Write three different number sentences the girls might have written.

   _____ + _____ + _____ = _____

   _____ + _____ + _____ = _____

   _____ + _____ + _____ = _____

5. Tell why the number sentences are different, but they have the same numbers and sum.

   _____

   _____

   _____

Use Properties of Operations: Add
Operations and Algebraic Thinking

Strategy It doesn't matter which order you write addition number sentences in, but check the story problem to make sure you have the right numbers.

6. Dora and Emma are playing a game. Dora scores 5 points and then, she scores 3 more points. Emma scores 3 points and then, she scores 5 more points. Which girl has the most points in all? Tell how you know.

_____

_____

_____

Test Tip

Make a ten first, and then, add the other number.

7. Tell how to add 8 + 2 + 8.

_____

_____

_____

8. Show how you know by drawing a picture.

9. Look at the picture below. Write two addition number sentences that go with the picture.

 + =

_____

_____

10. Choose the number sentences that have the same sum as 8 + 9.

Ⓐ 4 + 4 + 9

Ⓑ 9 + 8

Ⓒ 2 + 5 + 4

Ⓓ 4 + 9 + 4

11. Kyle sees 5 frogs + _____ turtles in the pond.

Lisa sees 3 frogs + _____ turtles in the pond.

Kyle and Lisa each see 8 animals in all.

Complete the number sentence to find how many animals Kyle sees in all.

5 + _____ = _____ animals

Complete the number sentence to find how many animals Lisa sees in all.

3 + _____ = 8 animals

_____

_____

_____

Find the Unknown Addend to Subtract
Operations and Algebraic Thinking

DIRECTIONS: Answer the questions.

Strategy — Use addition facts to solve subtraction problems. For example, to find the answer to $15 - 3 = \boxed{}$, use $3 + 12 = 15$.

EXAMPLE

Find $11 - 8 = \boxed{}$.

Use a known addition fact to find the difference.

Think: 8 and what number makes 11?

$8 + ? = 11$

$8 + 3 = 11$

So, $11 - 8 = 3$

Test Tip

If you know the addition fact, you can use it to find the difference.

1. What addition fact can be used to find the difference: $14 - 6 = \boxed{}$?
   (A) $14 + 6 = 20$
   (B) $5 + 8 = 14$
   (C) $6 + 6 = 12$
   (D) $8 + 6 = 14$

2. Tell how Jane can use an addition fact to find the difference of $10 - 6$.

   _____

   _____

   _____

Test Tip

When you subtract 9 or 10 from a number, add either 1 or 2 to the number to make 10. Then, add on the other number for the final sum.

3. Find $14 - 9$.

   _____

4. Explain how you found the answer.

   _____

   _____

   _____

5. Which differences can be found by using the addition fact $4 + 9$?
   (A) $13 - 9 = 4$
   (B) $9 - 5 = 4$
   (C) $9 - 4 = 5$
   (D) $13 - 4 = 9$

6. What addition fact can help you subtract $15 - 6$ and $15 - 9$. Why?

   _____

   _____

   _____

Find the Unknown Addend to Subtract
Operations and Algebraic Thinking

Strategy | Use addition and subtraction facts to solve problems. For example, $16 - 5 = 11$ is related to $16 - 11 = 5$ and $11 + 5 = 16$ is the same as $5 + 11 = 16$.

7. Complete the addition fact below.

$7 + 6 =$ _____

8. Write two subtraction facts to match the addition fact.

$13 -$ _____ $=$ _____

$13 -$ _____ $=$ _____

9. Use the numbers 7, 9, and 16. Write two addition facts and two related subtraction facts.

_____ $+$ _____ $=$ _____

_____ $+$ _____ $=$ _____

_____ $-$ _____ $=$ _____

_____ $-$ _____ $=$ _____

DIRECTIONS: Write a number sentence. Solve it.

10. Alberto puts 12 pennies in his bank. He gets 5 more pennies and puts them in his bank. How many pennies are in Alberto's bank now?

_____

11. There are 17 pennies in Alberto's bank. He gives 5 pennies to his brother. How many pennies are in Alberto's bank now?

_____

12. Write an addition word problem and a related subtraction word problem using the numbers 3, 6, and 9.

13. Write number sentences for your problems.

_____

_____

14. Choose which facts are related to $9 + 8 = 17$.

Ⓐ $8 + 9 = 17$

Ⓑ $17 - 8 = 9$

Ⓒ $17 + 8 = 25$

Ⓓ $17 - 9 = 8$

Math

Use Counting Strategies: Add and Subtract
Operations and Algebraic Thinking

DIRECTIONS: Answer the questions.

Strategy Relate addition and subtraction to counting. Count all objects and then, count on (add) or count back (subtract).

EXAMPLE

Jake wants to draw 2 more bubbles in the picture. How many bubbles will there be if Jake draws two more bubbles? Tell how you know.

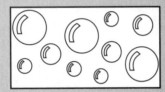

12 bubbles. You can count all the bubbles in the picture, and then, count on 2 more.

10, 11, 12

So, 10 + 2 = 12.

1. Charlotte drew these blocks to cut out for an art project. How many blocks are there in all?

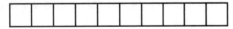

_____

2. Charlotte drew more blocks as shown below. Write and solve a number sentence to show how many blocks in all Charlotte now has.

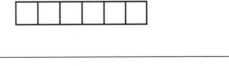

_____

_____

Test Tip

Use strategies such as such as counting all, counting on, and counting back to add and subtract.

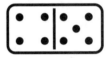

3. Choose the ways in which you can find how many dots are on the dot block.

(A) Start at 4 and count on 5 more.

(B) Start at 5 and count on 5 more.

(C) Start at 4 and count on 4 more.

(D) Start at 5 and count on 4 more.

4. Akio says he can subtract 2 from 14 by starting with 14 and _____.

(A) counting forward 2

(B) counting forward 14

(C) counting back 2

(D) counting back 14

Math

Use Counting Strategies: Add and Subtract
Operations and Algebraic Thinking

Strategy   Write number lines, number sentences, or count out loud to solve problems.

Test Tip   Re–read each problem and answer to be sure you have followed the directions.

5. Which picture makes this number sentence true?

5 apples + ☐ apples = 9 apples

Ⓐ   🍎 🍎 🍎 🍎

Ⓑ   🍎 🍎 🍎

Ⓒ   🍎 🍎 🍎 🍎 🍎

Ⓓ   🍎 🍎 🍎 🍎 🍎 🍎

6. Write a number to finish each sentence.

a. 1 more than 47 is _____.

b. 2 less than 23 is _____.

c. 1 less than 60 is _____.

d. 2 more than 35 is _____.

7. Daria solves a math problem by counting out loud. She counts. "5, 6, 7, 8, 9, 10, 11, 12."
Write a number sentence that Daria could be solving.

_____ ☐ _____ = _____

8. Leo uses a number line to solve a math problem. He starts at number 17 and counts back. He stops at number 9. Write a number sentence with its answer to show the problem that Leo is solving.

_____ ☐ _____ = _____

9. Lydia starts at a number and counts up to 19. Which number sentences can Lydia write to show her work?

Ⓐ 7 + 6 = ☐

Ⓑ 10 + 9 = ☐

Ⓒ 12 + 7 = ☐

Ⓓ 5 + 14 = ☐

10. Write count up or count back for each number sentence.

9 + 9 = ☐   _____

14 − 3 = ☐   _____

6 + 6 = ☐   _____

9 − 9 = ☐   _____

Name _____ Date _____

Math

Solve Problems: Use Addition and Subtraction Strategies

Operations and Algebraic Thinking

DIRECTIONS: Answer the questions.

Strategy   As you read each problem, choose a strategy: counting all, counting on, or counting back to add and subtract.

EXAMPLE

Tara wants to solve this problem: Two bunnies are sitting in the yard. Five more bunnies hop into the yard. How many bunnies are in the yard now?

Tara can count on to find how many bunnies.

Answer: Start at 2 and count on 5 more, "3, 4, 5, 6, 7."

$2 + 5 = 7$

There are 7 bunnies in the yard now.

1. Which two pairs are equal?

Ⓐ [3 + 4] and [5 + 2]

Ⓑ [16 − 8] and [9 + 9]

Ⓒ [6 + 7] and [15 − 2]

Ⓓ [2 + 10] and [8 + 3]

2. Fill in each box with one of the numbers below to complete each number sentence. Use each number only once. You will not use one number.

2	4	6	7	9

a. $9 + \boxed{} = 16$

b. $10 - 1 = \boxed{}$

c. $\boxed{} + 8 = 12$

d. $\boxed{} - 3 = 3$

3. Write three different number sentences using only the numbers in the box below. Use ◯ to fill in the operation sign.

4	5	6	9	11	10	15

_____ ◯ _____ = _____

_____ ◯ _____ = _____

_____ ◯ _____ = _____

4. Marco's model plane is 6 inches long. Kyle's model plane is 14 inches long. How much longer is Kyle's model plane than Marco's?

_____

Write how you know.

_____

_____

_____

_____

_____

Math

68

Math

Solve Problems: Use Addition and Subtraction Strategies

Operations and Algebraic Thinking

Strategy | Ask questions in words to help you solve problems. For example, for 7 + ☐ =14 you can ask *What number plus 7 makes 14?*

Test Tip | Read all of the answer choices before you choose your answer.

---

5. There are 15 birds on a fence. 6 birds fly away. How many birds are on the fence now?

   (A) 6

   (B) 9

   (C) 11

   (D) 15

6. Which shows a way to add 8 + 7?

   (A) 10 + 7

   (B) 4 + 4 − 2

   (C) 10 + 7 + 2

   (D) 10 + 7 − 2

   Write how you know.

   _____

   _____

7. Frieda reads her book for 11 minutes. Eli reads his book for 8 minutes. What is the total number of minutes that Frieda and Eli read?

   _____

   Write how you know.

   _____

   _____

8. Tan says he can solve this problem by using addition. Is Tan correct? Show how you know.

   A sunflower plant was 11 inches tall. Now it is 19 inches tall. How much has the plant grown?

   _____

   _____

   _____

9. Tammy gives 18 markers to Penny. Penny gives 4 markers to Billy and 2 markers to Sammy. How many markers does Penny have now?

   (A) 10

   (B) 6

   (C) 12

   (D) 2

   Write how you know.

   _____

   _____

   _____

10. Jill has 9 plants. She has room for 7 more plants her garden. How many plants can Jill put in her garden?

    _____

    _____

    Write how you know.

    _____

    _____

Solve Equations with an Unknown: Add and Subtract

Operations and Algebraic Thinking

DIRECTIONS: Answer the questions.

Strategy — Balance equations by making equal quantities on both sides of the equal sign.

Test Tip — The equal sign, =, means that the left side of the equation has the same value as the right side of the equation.

EXAMPLE

Which equation is true and which is false?

$5 + 6 = 11$

The sum of 5 and 6 is 11, so this equation is true.

$5 + 4 = 3 + 7$

The sum of 5 and 4 is 9. The sum of 3 and 7 is 10.

So, this equation is false, or not equal.

1. Choose the equations that are true.

   (A) $8 = 8$

   (B) $9 + 1 = 5 + 5$

   (C) $12 - 4 = 5 + 7$

   (D) $5 + 1 = 4 + 2$

2. Write if each equation is true or false.

   $14 = 6 + 8$ _____

   $17 - 9 = 6 + 3$ _____

   $5 + 3 = 7 + 1$ _____

   $9 - 1 = 5 + 3$ _____

3. Trevor says that the equation below is not true because the first part has 3 numbers. Is Trevor correct?

   $7 + 2 + 3 = 12 - 0$

   _____

Show how you know.

_____

_____

Test Tip

Look carefully at the operation signs when you read equations.

4. What number makes each equation true? Write the number in the box.

   $7 + 2 = \boxed{}$

   $12 + \boxed{} = 13$

   $\boxed{} = 16 - 9$

   $\boxed{} - 2 = 8$

Math

Solve Equations with an Unknown:
Add and Subtract
Operations and Algebraic Thinking

Strategy   Use addition and subtraction facts to help you balance equations.
For example, $9 + 8 = 17$ is the same as $17 - 9 = 8$.

5. Yun had 8 apples. He and his sister ate some of the apples. Now there are 5 apples. Write an equation that shows how many apples Yun and his sister ate.

_____

_____

6. Solve your equation. Tell how many apples Yun and his sister ate.

_____

_____

_____

7. Fill in the blanks. Make two true equations.

_____ + _____ = _____ + _____

_____ – _____ = _____ + _____

8. Write the number in the blank to make the equation true. Then, write a story problem that can be solved using the equation.

$5 +$ _____ $= 11$

_____

_____

_____

_____

_____

9. Which equations need a number greater than 6 in the blank to be true? Choose all that apply.

Ⓐ $13 -$ _____ $= 5$

Ⓑ $5 + 2 =$ _____

Ⓒ _____ $- 3 = 2$

Ⓓ $3 +$ _____ $= 13$

Show how you know.

_____

_____

10. Which equations need a number less than 4 in the blank to be true? Choose all that apply.

Ⓐ $9 -$ _____ $= 4$

Ⓑ $1 + 2 =$ _____

Ⓒ _____ $- 1 = 1$

Ⓓ $3 +$ _____ $= 4$

Show how you know.

_____

_____

_____

Name _____ Date _____

Math

Count to 120
Number and Operations in Base 10

DIRECTIONS: Answer the questions.

Strategy — Count on using ones, and then using tens for two–digit numbers. For example, counting on 3 from the number 38 is 39 (three tens, 9 ones) and 40 (4 tens and 0 ones).

Test Tip — It helps to say the numbers aloud as you count.

Count on ones by writing the missing numbers in the blanks.

47 ___ 49 50 ___ ___ ___ 54 ___ 56 ___ 58

The missing numbers in order are:
48, 51, 52, 53, 55, 57

3. Here is one ◯. Draw 26 ◯.

1. Count by 1s. Fill in the missing numbers.

		78		80	81	

114			117			120

2. Which number is the same as the word in the box?

five

- (A) 5
- (B) 7
- (C) 15
- (D) 55

4. Write the number that matches the number of squares shown.

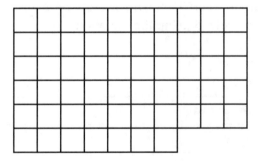

Count to 120
Number and Operations in Base 10

Strategy For numbers over 100, find the hundreds, tens, and ones. Say the number 523 in words: five hundreds, two tens, and three ones. Then, you can count by hundreds, tens, and ones.

Test Tip Look carefully at the operation signs when you look at equations.

5. Luka is counting his model cars. He has already counted 35 cars. He has 5 more cars to count. Which group of numbers shows how he counted the rest of his cars?

   (A) 40, 45, 50, 55, 60

   (B) 36, 38, 40, 42, 44

   (C) 36, 37, 38, 39, 40

   (D) 45, 55, 65, 75, 85

6. Pedro collects sports cards. He is counting his cards by ones. He says the number "112." But, Pedro has 5 more cards to count. When he finishes counting his cards, Pedro says he has 119 cards. Is Pedro correct?

   _____

   Show how you know.

   _____

   _____

   _____

   _____

7. Which groups of numbers are not in the correct counting order? Choose all that apply.

   (A) 89, 88, 87, 90, 91

   (B) 78, 79, 80, 81, 82

   (C) 89, 87, 88, 91, 92

   (D) 79, 80, 81, 82, 83

8. Myra has 31 books on her bookshelf. Jorge has 25 books on his bookshelf. Jorge says he needs 6 more books to have the same number of books as Myra. Count by ones to see if Jorge is correct. Write the numbers on the blanks.

   25

   _____

   _____

   _____

   _____

   _____

   _____

   Is Jorge correct?

   _____

Understand Place Value: Tens and Ones
Number and Operations in Base 10

DIRECTIONS: Answer the questions.

> **Strategy** | Find the tens and ones in two–digit numbers. The number 78 is 7 tens and 8 ones.

> **Test Tip** | Count how many tens and then, count how many ones.

EXAMPLE

Which number shows 1 ten and 7 ones?

Tens	Ones
1	7

(A) 1
(B) 7
● 17
(D) 71

1. Count the blocks. How many tens and ones are there?

_____ tens _____ ones

2. Write the number represented by the blocks.

_____

3. Which number means 2 tens + 8 ones?

(A) 18
(B) 82
(C) 28
(D) 8

4. How many tens and ones are in 53?

(A) 50 tens, 30 ones
(B) 5 tens, 3 ones
(C) 3 tens, 5 ones
(D) 50 tens, 3 ones

5. Look at the two numbers. Are they the same or are they different?

12 21

_____

Write how you know.

_____

_____

_____

_____

Understand Place Value: Tens and Ones
Number and Operations in Base 10

Strategy   Use blocks, objects, or drawings to understand place value. For example, for the number 86, draw 8 boxes of tens and 6 boxes of ones.

6. **What number do the blocks show?**

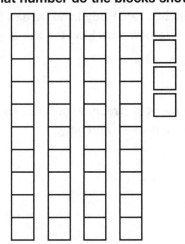

_____

7. **Which two numbers have more tens than the number 67?**

   Ⓐ 70

   Ⓑ 61

   Ⓒ 87

   Ⓓ 59

8. **Elena and Carmen are picking flowers. Elena picks 32 flowers. Carmen picks the number of flowers that has 1 ten more than 32. What number of flowers could Carmen have picked?**

_____

   Write how you know.

_____

_____

_____

_____

9. **Jeremy drew these circles. He said he drew 30 circles. Tell if Jeremy is correct and why.**

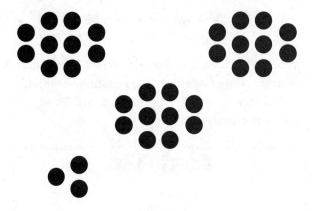

_____

_____

_____

_____

_____

_____

Compare Numbers
Number and Operations in Base 10

DIRECTIONS: Answer the questions.

Strategy — Compare two–digit numbers based on meanings of tens and ones digits. Identify which number is greater using tens and ones.

EXAMPLE

Compare these two numbers: 58 ____ 56.

Answer: 58 > 56

58 has 5 tens and 8 ones. 56 has 5 tens and 6 ones. They have the same number of tens, but 58 has more ones than 56. So, 58 is greater than 56.

Test Tip

< means less than
> means greater than
= means equal to

Which number is less than 71? Choose the best answer.

● 70
Ⓑ 73
Ⓒ 84
Ⓓ 92

1. Adia jumped rope for 43 seconds. Zahra jumped rope for 46 seconds. Who jumped rope for more seconds?

_____

Write how you know.

_____

_____

_____

2. Hector is 51 inches tall. Rudy is 55 inches tall. Write <, >, or = to compare how tall the boys are.

51 ____ 55

3. Write two numbers between 46 and 56. Then, tell which number is greater and why.

4. Compare the numbers. Write <, >, or = in the ☐.

65 ☐ 61

31 ☐ 31

58 ☐ 85

26 ☐ 28

Compare Numbers
Number and Operations in Base 10

Strategy Look at the tens place first to identify the greater number. Then, look at the ones place. For example, 56 > 55 but 56 < 66.

5. **Change the order of the numbers and rewrite them using < or >.**

   44 > 41   _____

   31 > 24   _____

   48 < 81   _____

   21 < 34   _____

6. **Write a number on the lines that makes these statements true.**

   62 > _____

   30 < _____

   _____ > 58

7. **Ming and Rosa are playing a game. Ming scores 38 points. Rosa scores less points than Ming. Write a number on the line that can be Rosa's score.**

   _____ < 38

   Show how you know. Use words, numbers or pictures.

Test Tip

Always know which way the signs go by remembering this: small < BIG
                                          BIG > small

8. **Choose two numbers that could complete the statement 56 > _____.**

   (A) 65

   (B) 56

   (C) 49

   (D) 55

9. **Write a number on the line so that this statement is true.**

   67 < _____

   What numbers can be written on the line so the statement is NOT true?

   67 < _____

Add Within 100
Number and Operations in Base 10

DIRECTIONS: Answer the questions.

Strategy — Add using models, place value, properties of operations, and the relationship between addition and subtraction.

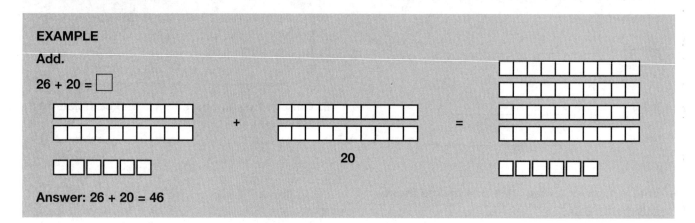

EXAMPLE

Add.

26 + 20 = ☐

Answer: 26 + 20 = 46

1. Jana has a box of 36 crayons. Later, she bought a box of 6 crayons. Draw a picture to show how many crayons Jana has in all. Use ⬚⬚⬚⬚⬚⬚⬚⬚⬚ to show tens and ☐ to show ones.

How many crayons does Jana have in all?

_____ crayons

2. Marco has 36 dog stickers. Ana has 10 bird stickers. How many stickers do they have in all?

Ⓐ 36
Ⓑ 37
Ⓒ 46
Ⓓ 73

3. 21 children went down a giant slide. Then, 5 more children went down. How many children in all went down the slide?

Ⓐ 21
Ⓑ 26
Ⓒ 56
Ⓓ 71

4. Maya has 23 green marbles. Jin has 6 blue marbles. How many marbles do Maya and Jin have total?

_____ + _____ = ☐ marbles

Test Tip

To check that you are using the correct operation, circle the operation sign in each problem.

5. Choose which number sentences have a total of 37.

Ⓐ 27 + 10 = ☐
Ⓑ 28 + 9 = ☐
Ⓒ 30 + 10 = ☐
Ⓓ 17 + 20 = ☐

Add Within 100
Number and Operations in Base 10

Strategy When adding numbers greater than 99, add hundreds to hundreds, tens to tens, and ones to ones. Keep place value in mind as you add.

6. Jacki counted butterflies for two days. On the first day she counted 8 butterflies. On the next day she counted 26 more butterflies than on the first day. How many butterflies did Jacki count the next day?

_____

Use words, numbers, or pictures to show how you got your answer.

Test Tip

Remember to add tens to tens and ones to ones.

7. Bella caught 6 fish. Then, she caught 11 more fish. To find the total fish that she caught, Bella wrote and solved this addition problem.

```
  11
+  6
  71
```

Tell what error Bella made. Then, write the correct answer.

8. Mario and his father made 12 blueberry muffins and 3 raisin muffins. Mario says he can count on by tens to find how many muffins they made in all. Is Mario correct? Tell why or why not.

How many muffins did they make in all?

_____

9. Mike knows how to play 12 songs on the piano. He will learn how to play 8 more songs this week. Can you use this addition problem to find out how many songs Mike will know how to play?

```
  12
+  8
   9
```

_____

Write how you know.

_____
_____
_____
_____

Math

Use Mental Math: Find 10 More or 10 Less
Number and Operations in Base 10

DIRECTIONS: Answer the questions.

Strategy Use addition and subtraction facts to help you add or subtract tens mentally. For example, to solve 43 – 10 = 30 mentally, know that 44 is 4 tens and 4 ones, and 10 is one ten and 0 ones. One ten from 4 tens and 4 ones is 30 tens and 4 ones.

EXAMPLE

There are 34 apples in the bin. Kayla uses 10 apples to make a pie. How many apples are left in the bin?

Think: 3 tens less 1 ten = 2 tens

And 4 ones left over

So there are 24 apples left in the bin.

1. Use mental math. Write the number that is 10 less and 10 more.

```
_____ 17 _____
10 less     10 more

_____ 38 _____
10 less     10 more

_____ 62 _____
10 less     10 more

_____ 89 _____
10 less     10 more
```

2. Which number is 10 more than 13?
   - (A) 33
   - (B) 23
   - (C) 41
   - (D) 130

Write how you know.

_____

_____

_____

Test Tip

Read the question carefully. Try to think of an answer before you look at the answer choices.

3. Which number is 10 less than 75?
   - (A) 74
   - (B) 85
   - (C) 65
   - (D) 57

Write how you know.

_____

_____

4. Karl and Shelli each have some shells. Karl has 10 more than 56 shells. Shelli has 10 less than 76 shells. Karl says that he has more shells than Shelli. Is Karl correct? Tell why or why not. Use words, numbers, or pictures.

Use Mental Math: Find 10 More or 10 Less
Number and Operations in Base 10

Strategy Read each problem carefully and look for words that tell you if you are looking for *how many more* or *how many less*.

5. Dawn and Kelly have 10 more notebooks than Matt and Laura. Matt and Laura have 25 notebooks.

   Dawn and Kelly have 5 notebooks. They used this number sentence 25 − 10 = 5.

   Is this correct? Tell why or why not. Use words numbers, or pictures.

Test Tip

Read the directions carefully. This will keep you from making simple mistakes and having to redo your work.

8. Choose the two statements that are true.
   - (A) 56 is 10 more than 66.
   - (B) 87 is 10 less than 97.
   - (C) 23 is 10 more than 32.
   - (D) 41 is 10 less than 51.

6. Gino has 25 pennies. He spends 10 pennies at the store. How many pennies does Gino have left?

   _____ pennies

   How do you know?

   _____

   _____

9. Tam has 56 points in a game. This is 10 less points than Shara has. How many points does Shara have?

   _____ points

   Write how you know.

   _____

   _____

   _____

7. 67 children are at the park. 10 more children come to the park. How many children are at the park now? Choose the best answer.
   - (A) 77
   - (B) 76
   - (C) 57
   - (D) 68

   Write how you know.

   _____

   _____

   _____

Subtract Multiples of 10
Number and Operations in Base 10

DIRECTIONS: Answer the questions.

> ### Strategy
> Think out the problem in your head using place value to solve it mentally. For example, think *40 plus what number makes 50?* 4 plus 1 makes 5, so 40 plus 10 makes 50. This helps you solve 40 − ☐ = 50.

EXAMPLE

There are 40 cows in the field. 20 cows go to the barn. How many cows are still in the field?

Think:

40 − 10 = 30

30 − 10 = 20

Answer: There are 20 cows still in the field.

1. Fill in the missing number to complete each number sentence.

   80 − 10 = _____

   60 − 30 = _____

   70 − 20 = _____

   50 − 40 = _____

2. Erik wrote an answer of 30 for a subtraction problem. Choose the two problems that Erik could have solved.

   Ⓐ 50 − 20

   Ⓑ 30 − 10

   Ⓒ 80 − 50

   Ⓓ 40 − 30

   Write how you know.

   _____

   _____

3. Ali has 60 trading cards. She gives Garrett 20 of them. How many trading cards does Ali have left?

   _____

   Show how you know. Use words, numbers, or pictures.

> ### Test Tip
> Knowing subtraction facts can help you subtract tens mentally.

4. What is the difference of 80 and 60?

   Ⓐ 10

   Ⓑ 20

   Ⓒ 30

   Ⓓ 40

   Write how you know.

   _____

   _____

5. What is another way to show 70 − 40 = 30?

   _____

   _____

Subtract Multiples of 10
Number and Operations in Base 10

> ## Strategy
> Use place value to identify which numbers are greater. Identify the tens and ones, remembering that tens are always greater than ones.

6. Grant's coach has 40 baseballs at the beginning of the baseball season. Grant's team loses 20 of them at practice and 10 of them during games. How many baseballs does Grant's coach have at the end of the season?

   _____

   Write how you know.

   _____

   _____

7. Emma bought 40 balloons for a party. On the way home, 10 balloons popped. Write and solve a subtraction sentence to find how many balloons were left.

   _____ – _____ = [   ] balloons

8. Kyle says that the difference of 50 – 20 is greater than the difference of 5 – 2. Is Kyle correct?

   _____

   Write how you know.

   _____

   _____

   _____

9. Choose the two number sentences that have a difference of 30.

   (A) $50 - 30 =$ [   ]

   (B) $30 - 30 =$ [   ]

   (C) $70 - 40 =$ [   ]

   (D) $90 - 60 =$ [   ]

10. Lauren has 60 tomato plants. Lindsay has 40 tomato plants. How many more plants does Lauren have? Show your work. Use numbers, words or pictures.

11. Choose the two number sentences that have a difference of 40.

    (A) $90 - 50 =$ [   ]

    (B) $40 - 10 =$ [   ]

    (C) $50 - 20 =$ [   ]

    (D) $60 - 20 =$ [   ]

12. Amanda says that the difference of 80 – 40 is greater than the difference of 8 – 4. Is Amanda correct?

    _____

    Write how you know.

    _____

    _____

Order and Compare Lengths
Measurement

DIRECTIONS: Choose the best answer.

Strategy   Order and compare lengths indirectly by using a third object.

EXAMPLE

Compare how tall the football players are. Who is taller, Player A or Player B?

A   B

Answer: Player B is taller than Player A.

1. Jason has two pencils, Pencil A and Pencil B. He buys another pencil that is shorter than Pencil A but longer than Pencil B. Draw the pencil that Jason buys.

A

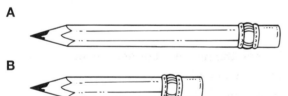

B

Test Tip

Check your answer to see if it makes sense.

2. **Look at markers L, M, and N. Which marker is the longest? Write how you know.**

L   

M   

N   

_____

_____

3. **Which shows the ladders in order from longest to shortest? Choose the best answer.**

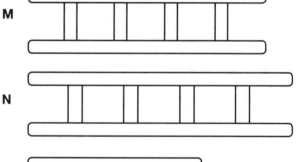

(A) M, N, P

(B) N, M, P

(C) P, M, N

Order and Compare Lengths
Measurement

Strategy Use many short objects to measure and compare lengths of longer objects.

4. **Which animal is the tallest? Choose the best answer.**

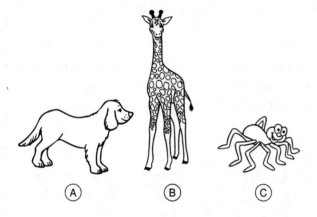

Ⓐ   Ⓑ   Ⓒ

5. **Look at the three boards below, labeled X, Y, and Z. Which shows the boards from shortest to longest?**

X
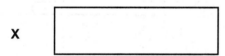

Y
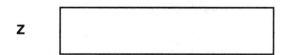

Z

Ⓐ X, Y, Z
Ⓑ Y, Z, X
Ⓒ X, Z, Y

6. **Amir planted some bean plants, as shown below. He says that plant J is the tallest. Is he correct? Write how you know.**

G   H   J

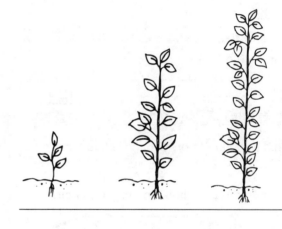

_____

_____

_____

_____

Measure Length
Measurement

DIRECTIONS: Choose the best answer.

> **Strategy** Measure lengths using multiple copies of one object to measure length of a larger object.

> **Test Tip** Make sure you understand what is being asked, and then, make sure your choice answers the question.

EXAMPLE

Look at the paper clips and the pencil. How many paper clips long is the pencil?

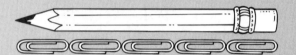

This pencil is about 5 paper clips long.

1. How many paper clips long is the pencil?

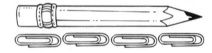

_____

2. Look at the fish and the bear. How many fish long is the bear?

_____

3. Use this paper clip to measure the pair of scissors below. About how many paper clips long is the pair of scissors? Choose the best answer.

(A) 2
(B) 3
(C) 4
(D) 5

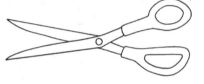

4. Look at Ladder A and Ladder B. Which ladder is longer?

A

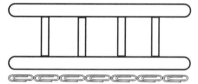

B

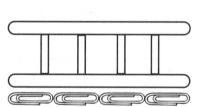

_____

Measure Length
Measurement

Write how you know.

_____

_____

_____

_____

_____

_____

5. Which spoons are longer than the spoon below?

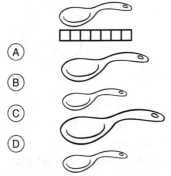

Ⓐ

Ⓑ

Ⓒ

Ⓓ

6. Jamie has two pieces of string. He needs the longest piece to tie around a package. Tell how he can decide which piece of string is the longest. Use words, numbers, or pictures.

7. Look at the fish and the cat. How many fish long is the cat?

_____

8. Grandpa is measuring a box to store his hat. What will he use to measure how long the box is?

Ⓐ

Ⓑ

Ⓒ

Ⓓ

Math

Tell and Write Time: Hour and Half-Hour
Measurement

Strategy   Identify clocks that are analog and digital and tell the time to the hour and half–hour.

Test Tip   Remember that on some clocks the short hand shows the hour and the long hand shows the minutes.

EXAMPLE

How are the clocks alike? Choose all that apply.

Clock A   Clock B

● They show the hour and the minutes.

● They show the same time.

Ⓒ They have an hour hand and a minute hand.

Ⓓ The time shown on Clock A is earlier than the time shown on Clock B.

Ⓔ The time shown is 3 o'clock.

The two clocks show the same time, 2:00, and show hours and minutes. So, A and B are correct. Only Clock A has an hour hand and a minute hand, so C is not correct. And because the time shown, 2:00, is the same for both clocks, D and E are not correct.

Test Tip

To help you tell the time on a digital clock, remember that the number for the hour is written first and the number of minutes past the hour are written next.

1. **Look at the digital clock below. Which clock shows the same time? Choose the best answer.**

Ⓐ   Ⓑ

Ⓒ   Ⓓ

2. **Clock A shows the time Channa went to the park. Clock B shows the time Yary went to the park. Channa says she and Yary went to the park at the same time. Is Channa correct? Tell why or why not.**

Clock A   Clock B

_____

_____

_____

_____

_____

Name _____   Date _____

Math

Tell and Write Time: Hour and Half-Hour
Measurement

Strategy   Apply the rules of time to clocks and count numbers from 1 to 12.

3. Which clocks show the time to the half hour?
Choose all that apply.

Ⓐ   Ⓑ

Ⓒ   Ⓓ

4. Write the time shown on the clock.

_____

5. Tam needs to leave for school at 7:00 in the morning. He looks at the clock below and says it is time to leave. Is Tam correct? Write how you know.

_____

6. Sonia starts lunch at the time shown on Clock A. She finishes lunch at the time shown on Clock B. Write the time Sonia starts lunch and the time she finishes lunch. Tell how you know you are correct.

Clock A   Clock B

_____
_____
_____
_____
_____
_____
_____
_____
_____

7. Look at the digital clock. Which analog clock shows the same time?

Ⓐ   Ⓑ

Ⓒ   Ⓓ

Represent Data
Measurement and Data

Strategy Collect and show data in drawings and charts to understand the information.

Test Tip To understand data in a table, read across the row and down the column.

EXAMPLE

Mrs. Park collected some data and organized it in a table. Mrs. Park asked students which exercise they like best. Five students like doing push–ups, 2 like pull–ups, and 6 like jump rope. Mrs. Park's table is shown below.

Favorite Kind of Exercise	
Exercise	**Number of Students**
Push–Ups	5
Pull–Ups	2
Jump Rope	6

1. **Mrs. George's students told the ways they get to school.**

   Jack, June, and Mark walk.

   Julia, Eva, Nora, and Teresa ride in a car.

   Rita, Jorge, Paul, Berta, Victor, and Leo ride a bus.

   Write numbers in the table below to show the data.

How We Get to School	
Walk	
Car	
Bus	

2. **Look at the table below. Some first grade students chose their favorite animal at the animal park.**

Favorite Part of Animal Park	Number
Monkeys	✓ ✓ ✓
Lions	✓ ✓ ✓ ✓ ✓
Tigers	✓ ✓ ✓ ✓

How many students chose each kind of animal?

_____

_____

_____

3. **Write in the table to show how many ▢ , ◯ , and ☆ in this group of shapes.**

▢ ◯ ▢ ☆ ☆ ☆ ☆ ◯ ▢

Shape	Number
▢	
◯	
☆	

Represent Data
Measurement and Data

Strategy Draw your own table and pictures to collect data to understand information in a word problem, and to solve word problems.

Test Tip Tables are made to make data easier to understand. Read the headings for each row and column to help you understand what data is shown in the table.

4. Kyle's baseball team packed the items they need for their next game. Which category had the most number of items?

Item	Number
⚾	4
🧢	9
🏏	4

Ⓐ baseball

Ⓑ cap

Ⓒ bat

5. Mrs. Sammi asked her students what kinds of pets they have. She wrote their names next to a picture of the kind of pet they have. How many students told the kind of pet they have? Choose the best answer.

Kind of Pet	Name of Student
🐕	Jana, Kyle, Leo, Kaitlyn, Van, Rosa, Jamil
🐟	Ali, Lisa, Maddie, Sitha
🐈	Tova, Aram, Juan, Isabel, Ana

Ⓐ 6

Ⓑ 4

Ⓒ 12

Ⓓ 16

6. Cam and Vilma count their coins. Then, they make a chart to show how many of each coin they have. They have the coins shown below.

How many categories will their chart have? Write how you know.

_____

_____

_____

Interpret Data
Measurement and Data

Strategy   Read the information in a table or drawing carefully and use the data to answer questions.

Test Tip   Read all the information in a table. If there are pictures, be sure you know what each picture represents.

Favorite Pizza Toppings	
🍕🍕	✓ ✓ ✓ ✓
🧀	✓ ✓ ✓ ✓ ✓ ✓
🫑	✓

1. How many people chose cheese as their favorite topping?

- (A) 7
- (B) 5
- (C) 13
- (D) 1

2. Which topping is the least favorite? Choose the best answer.

(A)

(B)

(C)

3. Do more people in all like cheese and pepper or pepperoni and pepper? Write how you know.

_____

_____

_____

DIRECTIONS: Look at the table. It shows the favorite kind of exercise chosen by some students. Use the table to answer question 4.

Favorite Kind of Exercise	
Exercise	**Number of Students**
Push–Ups	11
Pull–Ups	5
Jump Rope	7

4. How many more students like to do push–ups than pull–ups? Write how you know.

_____

_____

How many fewer students like to do pull–ups than jump rope? Show your work.

_____

_____

Interpret Data
Measurement and Data

Strategy   Read the top of each column to find out what kind of information is given in a table. Then, read the directions for each table carefully to know what information to find.

DIRECTIONS: Look at the table. It shows some students' favorite part of the animal park. Each ✓ = 1 student. Use the table to answer questions 5, 6, and 7.

Favorite Part of Animal Park	Number
Monkeys	✓ ✓ ✓
Lions	✓ ✓ ✓ ✓ ✓
Tigers	✓ ✓ ✓ ✓

5. How many students in all liked the lions and the tigers best? How do you know?

_____

_____

_____

_____

6. Which two animals were chosen by less than 5 students?

(A) monkeys

(B) lions

(C) tigers

7. Which two animals were chosen by more than 3 students?

(A) monkeys

(B) lions

(C) tigers

DIRECTIONS: Look at the chart. Mr. Samson asked some of his students how they get to school each day. They wrote their names on the chart next to how they get to school. Use the chart to answer questions 8 – 10.

How We Get to School	
Bus	Janice, Jon, Geraldo, Kim
Car	Marcos, Noel, Rita
Bike	Rosa, Jason, Felipe, Angela, Tran

8. How many students in all rode the bus or a bike?

_____

9. How many fewer students rode in a car than a bus?

_____

10. How many students in all rode the bus or in a car?

_____

Identifying Attributes of Shapes
Reason with Shapes and Their Attributes

Strategy — Learn and understand defining attributes and non–defining attributes of shapes to identify shapes of objects.

Test Tip — A defining attribute is a feature that applies to a shape, such as number of corners, number of edges, or if the edges are straight or curved. A non–defining attribute can apply to any shape, such as color and size.

EXAMPLE

Which picture looks most like a rectangle?

Ⓐ   ● 🍫 FRUIT BAR

Ⓒ   Ⓓ

1. Which shape is a rectangle? Choose all that apply.

Ⓐ   Ⓑ

Ⓒ   Ⓓ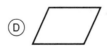

Test Tip

Count the number of corners and sides to help you name a shape.

2. What is the name of this shape? Write how you know.

_____

_____

_____

DIRECTIONS: Use the shapes below to answer questions 3–5.

E   F

3. Lila drew the shape that has no corners and one curved edge. Did Lila draw shape E or shape F? Write how you know.

_____

_____

4. Name the shape Lila drew.

_____

Identifying Attributes of Shapes
Reason with Shapes and Their Attributes

Strategy   Sort shapes into groups by identifying the attributes, or features, that are the same.

5. Tell why the other shape cannot be the shape Lila drew.

_____

_____

_____

6. Draw a square inside a triangle.

DIRECTIONS: Gayle wants to sort these shapes into groups. Use the shapes to answer questions 7–10.

Test Tip

Look carefully at the attribute of a shape. Even though the colors, sizes, or positions of one type of shape are different, the kind of shape does not change if it has the same number of corners and sides.

7. Gayle put all the circles in one group. How many circles are in the group?

_____

8. How many shapes have stripes? Name the shapes.

_____

_____

_____

9. How many shapes are white triangles?

_____

10. How many shapes are white?

_____

11. Choose the answer that describes the shape below.

(A) round with no corners

(B) four corners with straight sides

(C) three corners with curved sides

(D) one corner with round side

12. Describe a circle in your own words.

_____

_____

Compose Composite Shapes
Reason with Shapes and Their Attributes

Strategy | Create composite shapes from two-dimensional and three-dimensional shapes. Use sketches to help you visualize the new shape.

Strategy | A composite shape is a new shape made by combing multiple shapes, such as making a rectangle with two squares.

EXAMPLE

Which shape was used to make this shape?

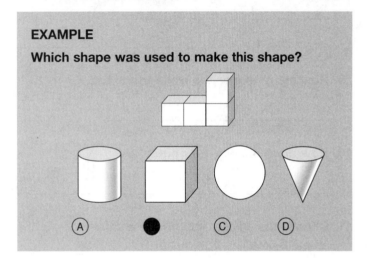

Ⓐ   ●   Ⓒ   Ⓓ

1. **What shapes will you have if you cut this shape in half? Choose the best answer.**

   Ⓐ two circles
   Ⓑ two squares
   Ⓒ two rectangles
   Ⓓ two triangles

   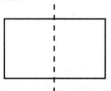

Test Tip

Imagine what each object looks like before choosing your answer.

2. **Choose the shapes that can be combined to make a square.**

   Ⓐ   Ⓑ

   Ⓒ   Ⓓ

3. **Nona said the shape below is a cube. Is Nona correct? Tell why or why not.**

   _____
   _____
   _____
   _____
   _____

4. **What three-dimensional shapes were used to make this new figure? Choose all that apply.**

   Ⓐ

   Ⓑ

   Ⓒ

   Ⓓ

Compose Composite Shapes
Reason with Shapes and Their Attributes

Strategy | Identify the attributes of single shapes that make up a composite figure. For example, does the shape have a round or straight edge? Flat or circle face?

5. Draw a new figure using these three shapes.

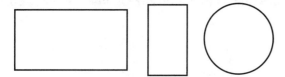

7. Which shape can fit into the first shape, A or B?

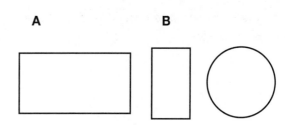

Write how you know.

_____

_____

_____

_____

_____

Test Tip

Count the number of corners and sides to help you name a shape.

6. Draw three straight lines inside this rectangle. What new shapes did you make?

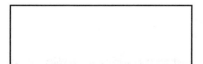

Partition Shapes into Equal Shares
Reason with Shapes and Their Attributes

Strategy — Understand that a whole is made up of two halves, four fourths, or four quarters and apply the rules of wholes to answer questions.

EXAMPLE

How many equal parts does this circle have? Name the parts.

Answer: The circle has 2 equal parts. Each part is called a half.

1. Owen divided this piece of paper into equal shares. How many equal shares does Owen's paper have? Choose the best answer.

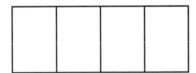

(A) 2
(B) 3
(C) 4
(D) 6

Test Tip

Look for key words in the directions, such as all or best. This will tell you if one answer or more than one answer is needed.

2. Akiko and Ella each ate half a pizza. Which picture shows half a pizza? Choose all that apply.

(A)    (B)

(C) 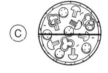   (D)

3. Ari, Nate, Jun, and Carlo shared a pie. They ate it all. They each got the same size piece. Draw a picture to show how they could have cut the pie.

4. Lisa cut out this paper circle. She drew a line down the middle to make two halves. She says that if she draws another line and makes four fourths, that the fourths will be the same size as the halves. Is Lisa correct? Write how you know.

_____

_____

_____

Partition Shapes into Equal Shares
Reason with Shapes and Their Attributes

Strategy   Ask yourself how many parts equal a whole to answer questions about dividing shapes into equal parts.

Test Tip   In questions that are grouped together, look for information in one question that may help you answer another question.

5. Toby wants to equally share a fruit bar with Alan. He cuts the bar into 2 pieces as shown below.

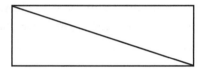

Will Toby and Alan each get an equal share? Tell how you know.

_____

_____

_____

6. Name each part of the bar.

_____

_____

7. How can Toby make another cut in the bar so he can share it equally with 2 more friends? Draw a picture to show your answer.

8. On Monday, David and his sister shared a small pizza. It was cut into 2 equal-size pieces. On Saturday, David shared the same-size pizza with three of his friends. This pizza was cut into 4 equal-size pieces. Did David eat more pizza on Monday or on Saturday? How do you know? Use words or pictures.

Strategy Review

In this section, you will review the strategies you learned and apply them to practice the skills.

Strategy Use basic operations to solve problems.

EXAMPLE

There are 3 cows, 4 horses, and 7 sheep in the field. How many animals are there in all in the field?

First, write a number sentence. Use a ☐ for the unknown number.

$3 + 4 + 7 = $ ☐

Next, change the order of the addends to make groups that are easy to add, like 3 and 7.

$3 + 7 + 4 = $ ☐

Now, add 3 + 7.

$3 + 7 = 10$

Then, add 10 + 4.

$10 + 4 = 14$

The number of animals in all is 14.

1. The sum of 7 + 6 is the same as the sum of
   _____. Choose three.

   Ⓐ $3 + 3 + 7$

   Ⓑ $6 + 7$

   Ⓒ $2 + 5 + 6$

   Ⓓ $7 + 8$

2. Jana saw 9 ants in a line. 4 ants marched into their ant hill. Write a number sentence to show how to find how many ants are left. Then, solve it. Use a ☐ for the number of ants that are left.

   _____

   _____

3. Hal solved this problem by writing and solving an addition number sentence.

   Ina has 14 sports cards. She gives 5 sports cards to Aaron.

   How many sports cards does Ina have left?

   Complete the number sentence to show how Hal solved the problem. Then, write how many sports cards Ina has left.

   _____ + 5 = 14

   Ina has _____ sports cards left.

4. Jan has 12 marbles. Gayle gives her 7 more. Jan and Gayle each write a number sentence to find how many marbles Jan has all together.

   Jan's Way: $12 + 7 = $ ☐ marbles

   Gayle's Way: $7 + 12 = $ ☐ marbles

   Which way is correct? Write how you know.

   _____

   _____

   _____

5. Solve each number sentence, and tell how many marbles Jan has all together.

   _____

   _____

Strategy Review

| **Strategy** | Read word problems carefully. Make sure you know what you are asked to do. |

EXAMPLE

6 ducks are swimming in the pond. 3 ducks fly away. How many ducks are left?

First, look for key words.

The question states: 3 ducks "fly away." The question asks "how many are left?"

Then, decide what operation you will use.

Use subtraction, because "fly away" means take away and so does "how many are left."

There are 3 ducks left.

1. There are 3 big fish and 2 small fish. How many total fish are there?

   (A) 1
   (B) 2
   (C) 3
   (D) 5

2. There are 6 yellow balls, 5 orange balls, and 8 green balls. How many balls are there in all?

   _____

EXAMPLE

There are 30 flowers. Shelly plants 10 more. How many flowers are there in all?

First, decide what operation you will use.

Use addition, because you are asked to find "how many in all."

Next, mentally add 10 more.

10 more than 30 is 40.

There are 40 flowers in all.

3. There are 25 apples on the tree. 10 apples fall to the ground. How many apples are left on the tree?

   (A) 35
   (B) 15
   (C) 10
   (D) 5

4. Trey is 48 inches tall. His older sister is 5 inches taller. How tall is Trey's older sister? Write how you know.

   _____

   _____

   _____

   _____

5. Tina's cat had 6 kittens. Tina's mom gave 3 kittens to her friend, 1 kitten to Tina's aunt, and 1 kitten to Tina's teacher.

   Write the number sentence that you can use to solve how many kittens Tina has left.

   _____

   Write how you know.

   _____

   _____

   _____

Strategy Review

Strategy Use what you know about numbers, shapes, and measurement to answer questions.

EXAMPLE

Write the missing numbers.

6, 7, _____, 9, _____, 11

First, think: One more than 7 is 8. Or, 1 less than 9 is 8.

Write 8 after 7 and before 9.

Then, think: One more than 9 is 10. Or, one less than 11 is 10.

Write 10 after 9 and before 11.

6, 7, 8, 9, 10, 11

1. Write the three missing numbers in the box.

| 78 | 79 | | 81 | | 83 | |

DIRECTIONS: Use the numbers in the box to write the missing numbers in questions 2–4. You will not use all the numbers.

57	91	118	87	58	53	93
115	121	62	59	90	94	120

2. 55, 56, _____, _____, _____, 60

Write how you know.

_____

_____

3. 88, 89, _____, _____, 92, _____

4. _____, 116, 117, _____, 119, _____

EXAMPLE

You can use a place–value chart to help you compare the numbers 34 and 37.

Tens	Ones
3	4
3	7

First, look at the tens. Compare them.

The tens are the same.

Next, look at the ones. Compare them.

4 ones are less than 7 ones.

Then, write <, >. or = in the ☐.

34 $<$ 37

5. Write the number that has 5 tens and 0 ones.

_____

6. Compare 67 and 42, Write <, >, or = on the line.

67 _____ 42

Strategy Review

Strategy	Choose the right tool and units to measure objects.

You can use rulers, meter sticks, and measuring tape to measure objects in inches, centimeters, meters, or feet. You can also measure objects with other objects. If you measure something in inches, you say it is a certain number of inches long. If you measure something in paper clips, you say the object is a certain number of paper clips long.

EXAMPLE

How many paper clips long is the spoon?

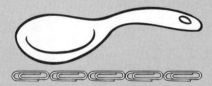

Count the paper clips, starting at the left.

The spoon is 5 paper clips long.

1. Freda has a straw that is 2 paper clips longer than the one below. How many paper clips long is Freda's straw?

(A) 2 paper clips

(B) 5 paper clips

(C) 7 paper clips

(D) 9 paper clips

2. Which leaf is the longest? Write how you know.

Leaf A   Leaf B   Leaf C

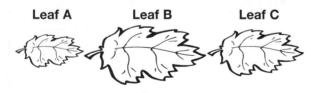

_____

_____

_____

Strategy

Use graphs, tables, and drawings to understand data.

EXAMPLE

The table shows the pets that some first grade students have.

Pets We Have	
Pet	**Number of Students**
Dog	8
Cat	3
Bird	1

How many more students have a dog than a bird?

First, find how many students have a dog.

8 students have a dog.

Then, find how many students have a bird.

1 student has a bird.

Finally, find the difference.

8 – 1 = 7. 7 more students have a dog than a bird.

3. Which pet do the most students have? _____

4. How many fewer children have a bird than a cat? Write how you know.

_____

_____

_____

Use Key Details
Reading: Literature

DIRECTIONS: Read the story. Then, answer the questions using details from the story.

Steve and his sister were playing. They were in the yard. A bird landed on the fence. They watched the bird fly to the ground. It picked up some grass. Then, it flew to a tree. Steve said the bird was making a nest.

Strategy — Ask yourself questions as you read to find key details: Who is in the story? What are the characters doing? Where are they? What happens?

Test Tip — Details tell about characters and what happens to them.

1. Who was with Steve?
   - (A) Steve's mother
   - ● Steve's sister
   - (C) Steve's dog
   - (D) Steve's friend

Which detail did you use to answer the question above?
   - ● "Steve and his sister were playing."
   - (B) "A bird landed on the fence."
   - (C) "It picked up some grass."
   - (D) "Then, it flew to a tree."

2. Write the key detail that tells where Steve and his sister were playing.

   They were in the yard.

3. Where did the bird land?
   - ● on the fence
   - (B) on the roof
   - (C) under the tree
   - (D) on Steve

Write how you know.

A key detail in the story is that a bird landed on the fence.

4. Write a question that uses the detail "It picked up some grass."

Possible Answer: How did Steve know the bird was making a nest?

5. Choose two key details that are missing from story.
   - (A) where Steve and his sister are playing
   - (B) what Steve and his sister see
   - ● the name of Steve's sister
   - ● if the bird was really making a nest

Write how you know.

They are important details that tell the reader more about the characters and the story events.

Use Key Details
Reading: Literature

DIRECTIONS: Read the story. Then, answer the questions using details from the story.

Get Warm
Brenda Butterfly was cold. She did not like it. She liked the sunny, warm weather. But it was fall. "What can I do to get warm?"
Her friend Buddy knew what to do. "I think you should follow the birds. They migrate. They fly to warm places in winter."
Brenda liked the idea. "That sounds great! Will you come with me, Buddy?"
They followed a flock of birds. It was a long trip. But it was so warm and sunny! Brenda and Buddy smiled. What a good idea!
There were many butterflies in this place. The flowers were colorful. Maybe Brenda and Buddy would stay.

Strategy — Look for one detail at a time as you reread: details about who is in the story, details about where the story takes place, and finally details about what happens to the characters in the story.

Test Tip — Read directions and each question carefully so you know how to answer. Sometimes, you choose an answer, write your own answer, or complete a sentence.

6. Brenda did not like _____.
   - (A) sunny weather
   - ● being cold
   - (C) her friend Buddy
   - (D) birds

Write how you know.

Possible Answer: Two key details in the story are that Brenda was cold and that she did not like being cold.

7. Buddy thought Brenda should migrate. Choose three details from the story that tell what migrate means.
   - ● "They fly to warm places in winter."
   - (B) "Brenda liked the idea."
   - ● "They followed a flock of birds."
   - ● "It was a long way."

8. Write the reason that Buddy tells Brenda to migrate. Why did he tell her to leave?

Possible Answer: It was cold where they lived.

9. Who did Brenda ask to go with her?
   - (A) her sister
   - (B) some birds
   - ● her friend Buddy
   - (D) nobody

Write how you know.

Possible Answer: A key detail in the story is that Brenda asked Buddy to come with her.

Describe Story Elements
Reading: Literature

DIRECTIONS: Read the story. Then, answer the questions using details from the story.

The New Puppy
My name is Matt. Today is my birthday. I am seven years old. I asked my mom and dad for a puppy for my birthday. They told me I am too little to take care of a puppy. But I think I can do it. I can walk the puppy. I can feed the puppy. I can love the puppy. I hope I get a puppy today!
The house is ready for Matt's birthday party. There are red, yellow, and blue balloons. There are streamers. There is a sign that says, "HAPPY BIRTHDAY, MATT!" I am Matt's mom. Matt is so excited for his birthday. All of his friends and family are here. We will have a great time.
"Matt! It is time to open your gifts!" I call over the music. Matt comes running into the room. He is smiling. He is excited. He opens all of his gifts. He gets a new racecar. He gets a new sweater. He did not get a puppy. "Mom, is there anything else?" he asks me. Just then, Matt's dad comes in the room. He has a blue leash in his hand. There is a puppy at the end of the leash. "Happy Birthday, Matt!" we both say. The puppy barks.

Strategy — As you read, identify the story parts—the characters, where the characters are, and what the characters do.

Test Tip — Stories have characters, setting, and events. Characters are the people or animals in the story. The setting is where the story takes place. Events are what happens to characters.

1. Who is having a birthday in the story?
   - (A) Matt's mom
   - (B) Matt's dad
   - ● Matt
   - (D) Matt's puppy

Write how you know.

Possible Answer: A key detail in the story is that today is Matt's birthday.

2. Write the key detail that tells where Matt is having his birthday party.

"The house is ready for Matt's birthday party."

3. Who is telling the story at the beginning?

Matt

Write how you know.

Possible Answer: The first sentence is, "My name is Matt."

4. Write a question that uses the key detail "All of his friends and family are here."

Possible Answer: Who is at Matt's birthday party?

Describe Story Elements
Reading: Literature

DIRECTIONS: Read the story. Then, answer the questions using details from the story.

adapted from *The Tale of Peter Rabbit*
by Beatrix Potter
Once upon a time there were four little rabbits. Their names were Flopsy, Mopsy, Cotton-tail, and Peter. They lived with their mother. They lived under the root of a very big fir tree.
One morning, Mrs. Rabbit said, "You may go into the fields. You may go down the lane. But don't go into Mr. McGregor's garden. Your father had an accident there. He was put in a pie by Mrs. McGregor."
"Now run along. And don't get into trouble. I am going out."
Then, Mrs. Rabbit took a basket and her umbrella. She went through the woods to the baker's. She bought a loaf of brown bread and five raisin buns.
Flopsy, Mopsy, and Cotton-tail were good little bunnies. They went down the lane to gather berries. But Peter was very naughty. He ran straight away to Mr. McGregor's garden. He squeezed under the gate!

Strategy — Read the story carefully. Then, retell the story to yourself to make sure you understand it.

Test Tip — To find the events in a story, ask yourself what happens to the characters.

5. Who is this story about?
   - (A) four foxes and their mother
   - ● four rabbits and their mother
   - (C) Mr. McGregor and his wife
   - (D) a baker

6. Write the key details that helped you answer the question above.

Once upon a time there were four little rabbits, and their names were Flopsy, Mopsy, Cotton-tail, and Peter. They lived with their mother underneath the root of a very big fir tree.

7. Write a key detail that tells what happened to the rabbits' father.

"He was put in a pie by Mrs. McGregor."

8. Write a question that uses the detail, "She bought a loaf of brown bread and five raisin buns."

Possible Answer: What did Mrs. Rabbit buy at the baker's?

9. Where did Flopsy, Mopsy, and Cotton-tail go?
   - (A) to the baker's
   - ● down the lane to gather berries
   - (C) to Mr. McGregor's garden
   - (D) to visit Mrs. McGregor

10. What is the setting of this story?
   - (A) in the city
   - (B) in the country
   - (C) under a tree
   - ● in the woods

Identify Sensory Words
Reading: Literature

DIRECTIONS: Read the sentences. Then, answer the questions.

Strategy As you read, look for words that describe using one of the five senses, such as *see* or *look*.

Test Tip Words that tell about using the senses are called *sensory details*. Your five senses include seeing, hearing, smelling, touching, and tasting.

EXAMPLE

The cat sleeps. His fur is soft. He purrs loudly.
Which word tells what sound the cat is making?
(A) sleeps
(B) soft
● purrs
(D) cat

1. The sun is hot. The clouds are puffy. The wind blows softly. I see a bird fly.
   Which sentences tell what you can see?
   (A) The sun is hot.
   ● The clouds are puffy.
   (C) The wind blows softly.
   ● I see a bird fly.

   Write how you know.
   Puffy tells how something looks. The word see is in the sentence.

2. Mom grows roses in the yard. The petals are big and red. Be careful with the stems. They are prickly!
   Write the words that describe using senses.
   big, red, prickly

Which senses do the words tell about?
seeing, touching

What other sense might tell about roses?
smelling

3. If a character was smiling and laughing while dancing on the beach, she feels *happy*.

4. Write the detail that helps you answer the question above.
   smiling and laughing; dancing

5. Choose the sentence that uses words that tell about feeling excited.
   (A) A dog walks slowly in the woods.
   (B) A blue fish jumps out of the water.
   ● The horse dashes like lightning down the lane.
   (D) The ball rolls on the grass.

Write the words that show feeling excited.
Possible Answer: The words dashes like lightning make it exciting.

11

Identify Sensory Words
Reading: Literature

DIRECTIONS: Read the words that tell about the senses. Then, answer the questions.

Strategy Categorize words, or put words that go together, into groups.

Test Tip Authors use words to tell, or to describe. As you read, picture in your mind what a word is describing. Use all of your senses.

EXAMPLE

Read the list. Then, write the words that tell about something cozy.

hard chair	Things that are cozy:
warm oven	1. soft bed
soft bed	2. thick blanket
stairs	
thick blanket	

6. Write the words that tell about something that has a loud sound in the sentence below.
   The fire truck screamed, its booming siren filling the street with noise.
   Possible Answers: screamed, booming, siren, noise

7. Read the list. Then, write the words that tell about something hot.

ice cream
soup
crackers
oatmeal
fruit
Foods that are hot:
1. soup
2. oatmeal

DIRECTIONS: Read the story. Then, answer the questions about the words in the story.

The rocket ship was <u>big</u>. It was as tall as a skyscraper! The engines <u>started</u>. The countdown began. The rocket flew up into the sky.

8. Choose two words that tell about the size of the rocket ship.
   ● large
   ● gigantic
   (C) small
   (D) tiny

Explain why the word *gigantic* is a better word to use than big.
Possible Answer: The story says the rocket ship is as tall as a skyscraper.

9. Which tells about the sound the rocket might make when it started?
   (A) shut down
   (B) ended
   (C) whispered
   ● roared

Which two sentences show that *roared* might be a better word to use than *started*?
   ● It describes the sound the engines make.
   ● It paints a picture in the reader's mind.
   (C) It means the same thing.
   (D) It is not a better word.

12

Identify Characters and Theme
Reading: Literature

DIRECTIONS: Continue reading from *The Tale of Peter Rabbit*. Then, answer the questions using details from the story.

Flopsy, Mopsy, and Cotton-tail listened to Mother. They did not go into Mr. McGregor's garden. They went to gather berries. But Peter ran to Mr. McGregor's garden and squeezed under the gate.

First he ate some lettuce and beans. Then, he ate some radishes. After that, he felt rather sick. So he went to look for some parsley.
But at the end of a cucumber frame, he met Mr. McGregor!
Mr. McGregor was on his hands and knees planting cabbages. He jumped up and ran after Peter. He waved a rake and called, "Stop thief!"
Peter was very scared. He rushed all over the garden. He had forgotten the way back to the gate!
He lost one of his shoes in the cabbages. He lost the other shoe in the potatoes.
After losing them, he ran on four legs and went faster. He may have gotten away if he had not run into a net and got caught by the large buttons on his jacket. It was a new blue jacket with brass buttons.

Strategy As you read, find details about how characters are alike and how they are different.

Test Tip Events are what happens to characters. Stories can have many characters. Make a list to help you remember them.

1. These events from the story are out of order. Write the numbers 2, 3, 4, 5, and 6 to retell *The Tale of Peter Rabbit*.
   [2] Peter eats lettuce and beans and radishes.
   [4] Peter forgets his way back to the gate.
   [5] Peter runs and loses his shoes.
   [1] Peter goes into Mr. McGregor's garden.
   [3] Mr. McGregor sees Peter in his garden.
   [6] Peter gets caught in a net.

   Write how you know.
   Possible Answer: The events are in order from first, next, and last.

2. How is Peter different from the other bunnies?
   (A) He is good and they are naughty.
   (B) He is white and they are brown.
   (C) He is fat and they are thin.
   ● He is naughty and they are good.

   Write how you know.
   Possible Answer: Peter was the only bunny who did not listen to his mother.

3. Choose the key detail that tells why Peter went to look for parsley.
   ● "After that, he felt rather sick."
   (B) "Mr. McGregor was on his hands and knees planting cabbages."
   (C) "Peter was very scared."
   (D) "He lost one of his shoes in the cabbages."

13

Identify Characters and Theme
Reading: Literature

DIRECTIONS: Finish reading *The Tale of Peter Rabbit*. Then, answer the questions using details from the story.

Peter was trapped in the net in Mr. McGregor's garden. Mr. McGregor was getting closer . . .
Peter gave up and began to cry. Some friendly birds flew to him. They begged him not to give up. Mr. McGregor tried to pop a bowl over Peter. Peter wriggled out just in time, leaving his jacket behind him.
Peter rushed into the tool shed. He jumped into a can. Mr. McGregor was sure that Peter was in the tool shed. He began to look under flowerpots. Suddenly Peter sneezed—'AH-choo! Mr. McGregor was after him in no time. Peter jumped out of a window. The window was too small for Mr. McGregor, and he was tired of running after Peter. He went back to his work.
Peter sat down to rest. He was out of breath and shaking with fright. He had no idea which way to go. Soon he began to wander around. He climbed up on a wheelbarrow. The first thing he saw was Mr. McGregor. His back was turned towards Peter. Beyond him was the gate!
Peter got down very quietly. He started running as fast as he could go. Mr. McGregor saw him at the corner. Peter slipped underneath the gate. He was safe at last in the woods outside the garden. Peter did not stop running or look behind him until he got home. He flopped down on the nice soft sand on the floor of the rabbit–hole and shut his eyes. His mother put him to bed and made him some tea. But Flopsy, Mopsy, and Cotton-tail had bread and milk and berries for supper.

Strategy Look for details that tell how characters' choices make events happen. Characters may choose to act a certain way. For example, Peter chooses to go into the garden.

4. Write two things you know about Mr. McGregor from this story
   Possible Answer: He likes to grow vegetables. He does not like rabbits in his garden.

5. Put a checkmark (✓) in each box to show which character the words describe.

	Peter Rabbit	Mr. McGregor	Flopsy, Mopsy, and Cotton-tail
Works hard in the garden		✓	
Lives under a tree	✓		✓
Did not listen to Mrs. Rabbit	✓		
Picked berries			✓
Chased Peter		✓	
Only got tea for supper	✓		
Had bread, milk, and berries for supper			✓

6. The story says that "Peter gave up and began to cry." Which two sentences from the story tell you why Peter decided not to give up.
   (A) "Peter gave up and began to cry."
   (B) "Peter sat down to rest."
   ● "Some friendly birds flew to him."
   ● "They begged him not to give up."

7. Mr. McGregor stops chasing Peter. What does this tell you about him? Use a detail from the story.
   Possible Answer: Mr. McGregor was tired after chasing Peter. He had work to do.

14

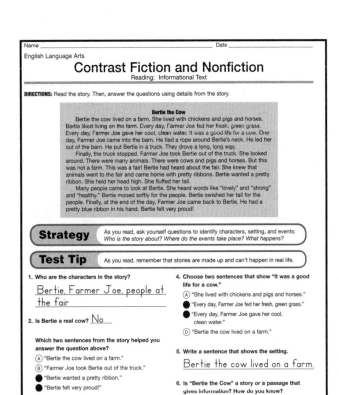

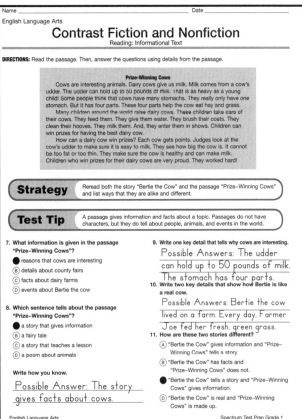

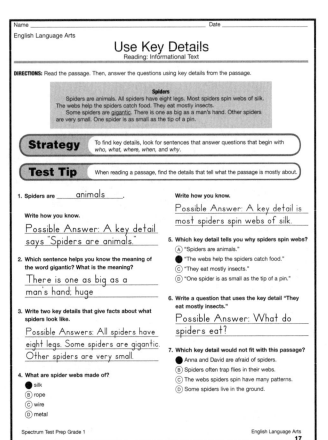

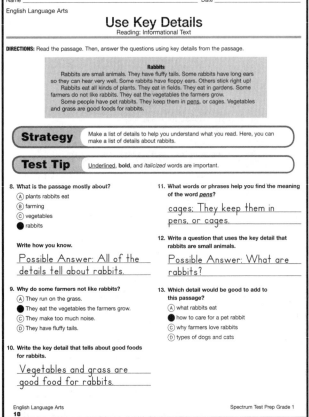

English Language Arts

Use Main Idea and Details
Reading: Informational Text

DIRECTIONS: Read the passage. Then, answer the questions using details from the passage.

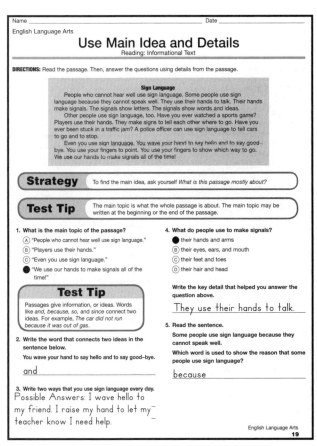

Sign Language

People who cannot hear well use sign language. Some people use sign language because they cannot speak well. They use their hands to talk. Their hands make signals. The signals show letters. The signals show words and ideas.

Other people use sign language, too. Have you ever watched a sports game? Players use their hands. They make signs to tell each other where to go. Have you ever been stuck in a traffic jam? A police officer can use sign language to tell cars to go and to stop.

Even you use sign language. You wave your hand to say hello and to say good-bye. You use your fingers to point. You use your fingers to show which way to go. We use our hands to make signals all of the time!

Strategy — To find the main idea, ask yourself *What is this passage mostly about?*

Test Tip — The main topic is what the whole passage is about. The main topic may be written at the beginning or end of the passage.

1. What is the main topic of the passage?
- (A) "People who cannot hear well use sign language."
- (B) "Players use their hands."
- (C) "Even you use sign language."
- ● "We use our hands to make signals all of the time!"

Test Tip

Passages give information, or ideas. Words like *and, because, so,* and *since* connect two ideas. For example, *The car did not run because it was out of gas.*

2. Write the word that connects two ideas in the sentence below.

You wave your hand to say hello and to say good-bye.

__and__

3. Write two ways that you use sign language every day.

Possible Answers: I wave hello to my friend. I raise my hand to let my teacher know I need help.

4. What do people use to make signals?
- ● their hands and arms
- (B) their eyes, ears, and mouth
- (C) their feet and toes
- (D) their hair and head

Write the key detail that helped you answer the question above.

__They use their hands to talk.__

5. Read the sentence.

Some people use sign language because they cannot speak well.

Which word is used to show the reason that some people use sign language?

__because__

English Language Arts

Use Main Idea and Details
Reading: Informational Text

DIRECTIONS: Read the passage. Then, answer the questions using details from the passage.

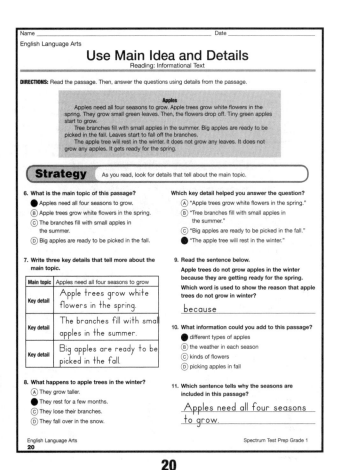

Apples

Apples need all four seasons to grow. Apple trees grow white flowers in the spring. They grow small green leaves. Then, the flowers drop off. Tiny green apples start to grow.

Tree branches fill with small apples in the summer. Big apples are ready to be picked in the fall. Leaves start to fall off the branches.

The apple tree will rest in the winter. It does not grow any leaves. It does not grow any apples. It gets ready for the spring.

Strategy — As you read, look for details that tell about the main topic.

6. What is the main topic of this passage?
- ● Apples need all four seasons to grow.
- (B) Apple trees grow white flowers in the spring.
- (C) The branches fill with small apples in the summer.
- (D) Big apples are ready to be picked in the fall.

7. Write three key details that tell more about the main topic.

Main topic	Apples need all four seasons to grow
Key detail	Apple trees grow white flowers in the spring.
Key detail	The branches fill with small apples in the summer.
Key detail	Big apples are ready to be picked in the fall.

8. What happens to apple trees in the winter?
- (A) They grow taller.
- ● They rest for a few months.
- (C) They lose their branches.
- (D) They fall over in the snow.

Which key detail helped you answer the question?
- (A) "Apple trees grow white flowers in the spring."
- (B) "Tree branches fill with small apples in the summer."
- (C) "Big apples are ready to be picked in the fall."
- ● "The apple tree will rest in the winter."

9. Read the sentence below.

Apple trees do not grow apples in the winter because they are getting ready for the spring.

Which word is used to show the reason that apple trees do not grow in winter?

__because__

10. What information could you add to this passage?
- ● different types of apples
- (B) the weather in each season
- (C) kinds of flowers
- (D) picking apples in fall

11. Which sentence tells why the seasons are included in this passage?

__Apples need all four seasons to grow.__

English Language Arts

Determine Meaning
Reading: Informational Text

DIRECTIONS: Read the question and answer choices. Choose the best answer.

Strategy — Use the other words in the sentence to find out which word to use. The other words in the sentence are clues.

Test Tip — Ask yourself questions about the missing word. For example, read this sentence. Anna added _____ to her cereal at breakfast. You can ask yourself, What do people add to cereal? (milk)

1. The bee flew to its _____. It went inside.
- (A) corner
- (B) cup
- ● hive
- (D) honey

Write a question that would help you find the answer for the question above.

__Possible Answer: Where do bees live?__

Test Tip

Use word parts to help you with the meaning of words. For example, the word part *re-* means "again." So, the meaning of replay is "to play again."

2. Harry _____ his shoes before taking them off.
- (A) tying
- ● unties
- (C) reties
- (D) tied

Write how you know.

__Possible Answer: I know that un- means "not." Harry's shoes are not tied if he is taking them off.__

3. I reread that book three times.

What does the word reread mean?
- (A) read one time
- (B) read first
- ● read again
- (D) did not read

Test Tip

You can also look for the root word in words to find meaning. The words cooks, cooked, and cooking all have the same root word—cook.

4. Sara <u>looks</u> at the painting for a long time.

What is the root word of the underlined word?

__Answer: look__

5. Pia is <u>sing</u> at the party tonight.

Which word has the ending that makes sense for the underlined word?
- (A) sings
- (B) singed
- ● singing
- (D) singer

English Language Arts

Use Text Features
Reading: Informational Text

DIRECTIONS: Read the question and answer choices. Choose the best answer.

Strategy — Use information in charts, lists, and pictures to help you understand a passage.

Test Tip — Many passages that give information include the following text features:
- table of contents: tells what page a topic or chapter starts on
- glossary: gives the meanings of words in the passage
- headings: titles of paragraphs

1. Read the table of contents below. Which chapter tells about making shoes?

Table of Contents

- (A) 1
- (B) 2
- ● 3
- (D) 4

2. On what page does the chapter about making shoes start?
- (A) 2
- (B) 4
- ● 8
- (D) 10

3. Read the glossary below.

GLOSSARY

Flower	the part of a plant that is colorful; the seeds of the plant are in the flower
Plant	to put a seed or flower into the ground to grow
Root	the part of a plant or flower that is in the ground; it gets food and water for the plant
Seed	a small object made by a plant that grows a new plant
Stem	a part of a plant that holds another part

What is a root?
- (A) the part of a plant that is colorful
- (B) to put a seed or flower into the ground to grow
- ● the part of a plant or flower that is in the ground
- (D) a small object made by a plant that grows a new plant

Which part of the plant holds the flower?

__stem__

Write how you know.

__Possible Answer: A stem is a part of a plant that holds another part.__

Name _____ Date _____
English Language Arts

Make Connections
Reading: Informational Text

DIRECTIONS: Read the passage. Then, answer the questions using details from the passage.

Strategy Make connections by finding what is the same and what is different about people, things, events, or places in a passage.

Test Tip As you read, look for details that show how the Fourth of July and Veterans Day are the same and how they are different.

American Holidays
We have many holidays in America. One fun holiday is the Fourth of July. Many people have parties on the Fourth of July. Many people watch fireworks shows. But why do we celebrate that day? The Fourth of July is the day we celebrate the birth of our country. America used to be ruled by England. A long time ago, soldiers fought for freedom. The Fourth of July is the day we celebrate that freedom.
Veterans Day is another important holiday. Veterans Day is a quieter holiday. It is the day to remember our soldiers. Soldiers fight to keep us free. They fight to keep us safe. The Fourth of July celebrates our freedom. Veterans Day celebrates the men and women who keep us free.

1. Which key details tell you why the Fourth of July is an important holiday?
 Ⓐ "Many people have parties on the Fourth of July."
 Ⓑ "Many people watch fireworks shows."
 ● "The Fourth of July is the day we celebrate the birth of our country."
 Ⓓ "America used to be ruled by England."

2. What do we celebrate on Veterans Day?
 soldiers

Write the key detail that helped you answer the question above.
 It is the day to remember our soldiers.

3. What two ideas are connected in this passage?
 Fourth of July and Veterans Day

4. Find 3 sentences in the passage that tell how the Fourth of July and Veterans Day are alike. Write the ideas in the graphic organizer.

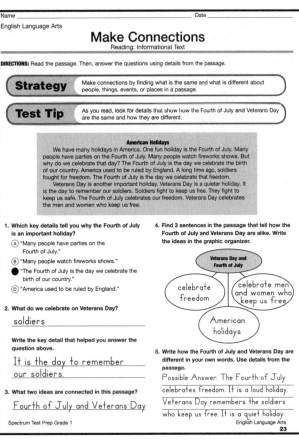

Veterans Day and Fourth of July — celebrate freedom — celebrate men and women who keep us free — American holidays

5. Write how the Fourth of July and Veterans Day are different in your own words. Use details from the passage.
 Possible Answer: The Fourth of July celebrates freedom. It is a loud holiday. Veterans Day remembers the soldiers who keep us free. It is a quiet holiday.

Name _____ Date _____
English Language Arts

Make Connections
Reading: Informational Text

DIRECTIONS: Read the passage. Then, answer the questions using details from the passage.

Strategy As you read, make a list of ideas and people. Then, write how they are alike.

Test Tip You can find details in the passage that connect firefighters and police officers— both people help others.

People Who Help
Firefighters are people who help. They work hard to keep us safe. They are very brave. Firefighters work long hours. Fires are very dangerous. Many firefighters get hurt in fires. Firefighters also help with traffic accidents. They make sure that all of the people around the accident stay safe.
Police officers are people who help, too. They keep us safe by making sure we follow the laws. If a person breaks the law, a police officer will take care of it. Police officers can also help if there is trouble. A police officer can help you if you are lost.

6. How are firefighters and police officers the same?
 Ⓐ They both fight fires.
 Ⓑ They both catch criminals.
 Ⓒ They both ride in fire trucks.
 ● They are both people who help.

7. Which key detail tells how firefighters help us?
 Ⓐ Firefighters are people who help.
 Ⓑ They not afraid of anything.
 Ⓒ Firefighters work very long days.
 ● They make sure people near an accident stay safe.

8. Write a key detail about police officers that shows how they are different from firefighters.
 Possible Answer: They keep us safe by making sure we follow the laws.

9. Who would you call if someone took your bike?
 a police officer

10. Who would you call to report a fire in the park?
 a firefighter

11. What other job would fit in this passage about people who help?
 Ⓐ student
 Ⓑ banker
 ● nurse
 Ⓓ baker

Name _____ Date _____
English Language Arts

Use Pictures
Reading: Informational Text

DIRECTIONS: Read the passage and look at the pictures. Then, answer the questions.

Strategy Compare the information given in the passage and in the pictures.

Test Tip Pictures and the words in the passage work together to give you all the information. Pictures may match the information in the passage. They may give more information to help you understand the passage.

EXAMPLE
Rabbits are small animals. Some rabbits are brown. Some rabbits are black. Rabbits have fluffy tails. Some rabbits have long ears. Other rabbits have floppy ears.

Put a checkmark (✓) to show if the key detail came from the passage or from the picture.

	From passage	From picture
Rabbits are small animals.	✓	
Rabbits have whiskers.		✓
Some rabbits are brown.	✓	
Rabbits can sit on their hind legs.		✓

1. Ethan is tired. He had a busy day. He went fishing. He went swimming. He went hiking. Now he is sleeping.

Put a checkmark (✓) to show if the key detail came from the passage or from the picture.

	From passage	From picture
Ethan is tired.	✓	
Ethan is camping.		✓
Ethan is in a tent.		✓
Ethan went swimming.	✓	

2. Horses are big animals. They can be brown. They can be black. Horses are very strong.

What new information about horses is shown in the picture?
 Horses eat grass.

3. Beth likes to go to the park. She likes to slide. She likes to jump.

Write a detail you learned from the passage and a detail you learned from the picture.
Passage
 Possible Answer: Beth likes to go to the park.
Picture
 Possible Answer: Beth likes to swing.

Name _____ Date _____
English Language Arts

Use Pictures
Reading: Informational Text

DIRECTIONS: Read each passage carefully. Then, choose the best answer for the question.

Strategy Ask yourself how the picture fits with the passage. What information does it give the reader?

Test Tip Use the picture as well as the passage to answer the questions.

EXAMPLE
Monkeys are funny animals. They can use their tails to hang from trees. They use their hands just like we do. Monkeys like to play.

Why can monkeys use their tails to hang from trees?
 ● Their tails are long.
 Ⓑ Their tails are short.
 Ⓒ Their tails are sticky.
 Ⓓ Their tails have glue.

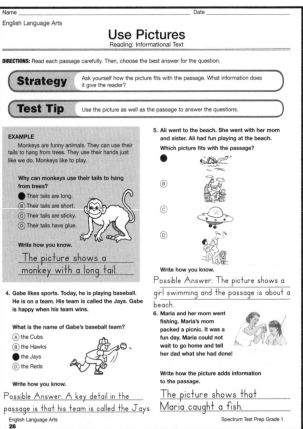

Write how you know.
 The picture shows a monkey with a long tail.

4. Gabe likes sports. Today, he is playing baseball. He is on a team. His team is called the Jays. Gabe is happy when his team wins.

What is the name of Gabe's baseball team?
 Ⓐ the Cubs
 Ⓑ the Hawks
 ● the Jays
 Ⓓ the Reds

Write how you know.
 Possible Answer: A key detail in the passage is that his team is called the Jays.

5. Ali went to the beach. She went with her mom and sister. Ali had fun playing at the beach. Which picture fits with the passage?
 ● (A)
 Ⓑ (B)
 Ⓒ (C)
 Ⓓ (D)

Write how you know.
 Possible Answer: The picture shows a girl swimming and the passage is about a beach.

6. Maria and her mom went fishing. Maria's mom packed a picnic. It was a fun day. Maria could not wait to go home and tell her dad what she had done!

Write how the picture adds information to the passage.
 The picture shows that Maria caught a fish.

English Language Arts

Compare and Contrast Two Texts
Reading: Literature and Informational Text

DIRECTIONS: Read the passages. Then, answer the questions using details from the passages.

> **Interesting Snakes**
> Snakes are interesting animals. Snakes live almost everywhere on Earth. Snakes live on land. Snakes live in water. Snakes do not live at the South Pole. Snakes can move without legs! They squeeze and stretch their muscles to slide across the land. Snakes do not have eyelids. They cannot blink. They cannot close their eyes to sleep. Snakes cannot see well. If you stand very still, a snake might not even notice you! Snakes are very interesting animals.
>
> **Dangerous Snakes**
> Snakes are very dangerous. Snakes can strike very fast. Some snakes eat small animals. They swallow them whole! Other snakes squeeze their prey. Other snakes have poison. They bite their prey. The poison can kill the prey. People must be careful in areas with snakes. If a snake is startled, it may bite you. Snakes are very dangerous animals.

Strategy — As you read, compare information that is the same and identify information that is different.

Test Tip — Reading two passages on the same topic can help you learn more about the topic.

1. What is the main topic of the first passage?
- ● Snakes are interesting.
- Ⓑ Snakes are dangerous.
- Ⓒ Snakes live almost everywhere on Earth.
- Ⓓ Snakes do not have eyelids.

Write how you know.
Possible Answer: The first sentence says that snakes are interesting animals.

2. Write the main topic of the second passage.
Snakes are very dangerous.

3. What is the same about the two passages?
Possible Answer: They are both about snakes.

4. Which two details show what the author of the second passage thinks about snakes?
- ● "People must be careful in areas with snakes."
- Ⓑ "Some snakes eat small animals."
- Ⓒ "If a snake is startled, it may bite you."
- ● "Snakes are very dangerous animals."

5. How are the two passages different?
- Ⓐ The first passage tells facts about snakes. The second passage tells opinions.
- ● The first passage tells snakes are interesting. The second author thinks snakes are dangerous.
- Ⓒ The first passage is made up. The second passage is real.
- Ⓓ The first author hates snakes. The second author loves snakes.

27

English Language Arts

Compare Two Texts
Reading: Literature and Informational Text

DIRECTIONS: Read the passages. Then, answer the questions using details from the passages.

> **Frogs**
> Frogs can live in many different places. They can live on the side of a mountain. They can live in the hot desert. They can live in rain forests. Frogs can live on land. They can live in the water. They can even live in trees!
>
> **Toads**
> Toads are a lot like frogs. Toads live in many places that frogs live. But, toads only live on land. They cannot live in the water. They cannot live in trees. Toads look a lot like frogs. A toad's body is fatter than a frog's body. Toads have shorter back legs. Toads are slower than frogs.

Strategy — Find reasons, or details, that tell how the author thinks about the topic. These reasons will help you find the main topic or main idea.

Test Tip — Reread both passages to find all of the information.

1. What is the main topic of the first passage?
- ● Frogs can live in many different places.
- Ⓑ Frogs are interesting.
- Ⓒ Frogs are nothing like toads.
- Ⓓ Frogs can live in trees.

Write how you know.
Possible Answer: All of the key details are about where frogs live.

2. Write the main topic of the second passage.
Toads are a lot like frogs.

3. What new information is given in the second passage?
information about toads

Write how you know.
Possible Answer: All of the key details compare toads to frogs.

4. Where can frogs live that toads cannot?
in the water; in trees

5. Which two key details in the passage "Toads" support the main idea?
- ● Frogs can live in water, but toads can't.
- Ⓑ Frogs can live on the side of a mountain.
- Ⓒ Frogs can even live in trees.
- ● Frogs can live in trees, but toads can't.

6. Which passage tells more about how frogs and toads are the same and different?
"Toads"

28

English Language Arts

Use Nouns and Verbs
Language

DIRECTIONS: Read the sentence and the word choices. Choose the best word or phrase to fill in the blank.

Strategy — Ask yourself what a noun names. Does it name a person, place, or thing?

Strategy — Identify words that name an action. Then, identify if the action is happening now, has already happened, or will happen in the future.

Test Tip — There are different kinds of nouns: common, proper, and possessive.

Test Tip — Possessive nouns have apostrophes and the letter s: Mary's.

Common nouns	Name a person, place, or thing: *cat, house, spoon*
Proper nouns	Name people or places: *Mike, Mrs. Jennings, The White House, Principal Green*
Possessive nouns	Show what belongs to a person, place, or thing: *Greta's bike, the park's playground*

Present verbs	Tells about an action that happened today: *I walk home. I cook dinner.*
Past verbs	Tells about an action that already happened: *I walked home yesterday. I cooked dinner on Monday.*
Future verbs	Tells about an action that will happened: *I will walk home tomorrow. I will cook dinner next week.*

1. _____ dog likes to run.
- Ⓐ Cara
- ● Cara's
- Ⓒ Girl
- Ⓓ Girls

Write how you know.
Possible Answer: The 's means that the dog belongs to Cara.

2. _____ new bike is bright red.
- ● Bill's
- Ⓑ Bills
- Ⓒ Bills's
- Ⓓ Bill

3. That room belongs to my brother. It is my _____ room.
brother's

4. The boat sinks into the water.
Which type of verb is used in this sentence, present, past, or future?
present

Write how you know.
Possible Answer: The 's means that the dog belongs to Cara.

29

English Language Arts

Use Nouns and Verbs
Language

DIRECTIONS: Choose or write the correct answer.

Strategy — Ask yourself how many nouns are in the sentence. Is only one person, place, or thing in the sentence? Is there more than one?

Test Tip — Nouns that are singular name one person, place or thing. They go with verbs that end in –s: The cat plays.

Test Tip — Proper nouns start with a capital letter.

5. For each common noun, write a proper noun on the line. Possible Answer:
dog	Sam
girl	Julia
teacher	Mr. Smith
school	King Elementary School

6. A caterpillar _____ leaves.
- Ⓐ eating
- Ⓑ eated
- Ⓒ eat
- ● eats

Test Tip — Nouns that are plural name more than one person, place or thing. Verbs do not have an –s at the end: The cats play.

7. The boys _____ at the ice rink in winter.
- Ⓐ skates
- Ⓑ skated
- ● skate
- Ⓓ skater

8. Write a sentence using each noun and verb.
friend, meet
Possible Answer: I meet a friend by the lake.

girls, walk
Possible Answer: The girls walk to the park.

9. Write the word correctly on the line.
The cat belongs to Leesa.
It is _____ Leesa's _____ cat.

10. Write a sentence that tells an action that you will do in the future.
Possible Answer: I will ride the bus.

30

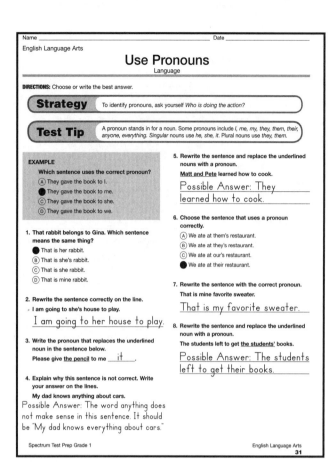

Name _____ Date _____

English Language Arts

Use Pronouns
Language

DIRECTIONS: Choose or write the best answer.

Strategy To identify pronouns, ask yourself *Who is doing the action?*

Test Tip A pronoun stands in for a noun. Some pronouns include *I, me, my, they, them, their, anyone, everything*. Singular nouns use *he, she, it*. Plural nouns use *they, them*.

EXAMPLE
Which sentence uses the correct pronoun?
(A) They gave the book to I.
● They gave the book to me.
(C) They gave the book to she.
(D) They gave the book to we.

1. That rabbit belongs to Gina. Which sentence means the same thing?
● That is her rabbit.
(B) That is she's rabbit.
(C) That is she rabbit.
(D) That is mine rabbit.

2. Rewrite the sentence correctly on the line.
I am going to she's house to play.
I am going to her house to play.

3. Write the pronoun that replaces the underlined noun in the sentence below.
Please give the pencil to me __it__.

4. Explain why this sentence is not correct. Write your answer on the lines.
My dad knows anything about cars.
Possible Answer: The word anything does not make sense in this sentence. It should be "My dad knows everything about cars."

5. Rewrite the sentence and replace the underlined nouns with a pronoun.
Matt and Pete learned how to cook.
Possible Answer: They learned how to cook.

6. Choose the sentence that uses a pronoun correctly.
(A) We ate at them's restaurant.
(B) We ate at they's restaurant.
(C) We ate at our's restaurant.
● We ate at their restaurant.

7. Rewrite the sentence with the correct pronoun.
That is mine favorite sweater.
That is my favorite sweater.

8. Rewrite the sentence and replace the underlined noun with a pronoun.
The students left to get the students' books.
Possible Answer: The students left to get their books.

Spectrum Test Prep Grade 1

English Language Arts
31

31

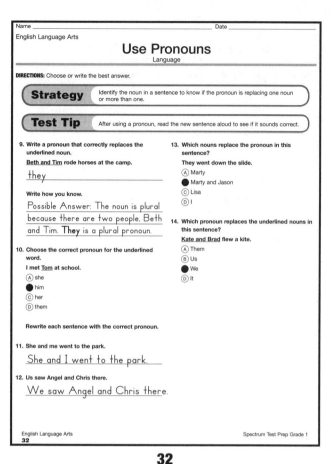

Name _____ Date _____

English Language Arts

Use Pronouns
Language

DIRECTIONS: Choose or write the best answer.

Strategy Identify the noun in a sentence to know if the pronoun is replacing one noun or more than one.

Test Tip After using a pronoun, read the new sentence aloud to see if it sounds correct.

9. Write a pronoun that correctly replaces the underlined noun.
Beth and Tim rode horses at the camp.
they
Write how you know.
Possible Answer: The noun is plural because there are two people, Beth and Tim. They is a plural pronoun.

10. Choose the correct pronoun for the underlined word.
I met Tom at school.
(A) she
● him
(C) her
(D) them

Rewrite each sentence with the correct pronoun.

11. She and me went to the park.
She and I went to the park.

12. Us saw Angel and Chris there.
We saw Angel and Chris there.

13. Which nouns replace the pronoun in this sentence?
They went down the slide.
(A) Marty
● Marty and Jason
(C) Lisa
(D) I

14. Which pronoun replaces the underlined nouns in this sentence?
Kate and Brad flew a kite.
(A) Them
(B) Us
● We
(D) It

English Language Arts
32

Spectrum Test Prep Grade 1

32

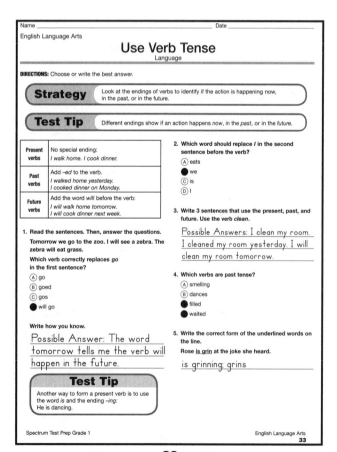

Name _____ Date _____

English Language Arts

Use Verb Tense
Language

DIRECTIONS: Choose or write the best answer.

Strategy Look at the endings of verbs to identify if the action is happening now, in the past, or in the future.

Test Tip Different endings show if an action happens *now*, in the *past*, or in the *future*.

Present verbs	No special ending: *I walk home. I cook dinner.*
Past verbs	Add *–ed* to the verb. *I walked home yesterday. I cooked dinner on Monday.*
Future verbs	Add the word *will* before the verb: *I will walk home tomorrow. I will cook dinner next week.*

1. Read the sentences. Then, answer the questions.
Tomorrow we go to the zoo. I will see a zebra. The zebra will eat grass.
Which verb correctly replaces *go* in the first sentence?
(A) go
(B) goed
(C) gos
● will go

Write how you know.
Possible Answer: The word tomorrow tells me the verb will happen in the future.

Test Tip
Another way to form a present verb is to use the word *is* and the ending *–ing*:
He is dancing.

2. Which word should replace *I* in the second sentence before the verb?
(A) eats
● we
(C) is
(D) I

3. Write 3 sentences that use the present, past, and future. Use the verb *clean*.
Possible Answers: I clean my room. I cleaned my room yesterday. I will clean my room tomorrow.

4. Which verbs are past tense?
(A) smelling
(B) dances
● filled
● waited

5. Write the correct form of the underlined words on the line.
Rose is grin at the joke she heard.
is grinning; grins

Spectrum Test Prep Grade 1

English Language Arts
33

33

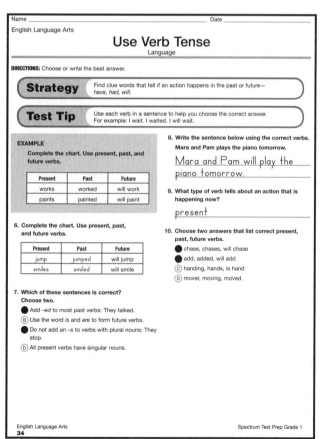

Name _____ Date _____

English Language Arts

Use Verb Tense
Language

DIRECTIONS: Choose or write the best answer.

Strategy Find clue words that tell if an action happens in the past or future—*have, had, will*.

Test Tip Use each verb in a sentence to help you choose the correct answer. For example: I wait. I waited. I will wait.

EXAMPLE
Complete the chart. Use present, past, and future verbs.

Present	Past	Future
works	worked	will work
paints	painted	will paint

6. Complete the chart. Use present, past, and future verbs.

Present	Past	Future
jump	jumped	will jump
smiles	smiled	will smile

7. Which of these sentences is correct? Choose two.
● Add *–ed* to most past verbs: They talked.
(B) Use the word *is* and *are* to form future verbs.
● Do not add an *–s* to verbs with plural nouns: They stop.
(D) All present verbs have singular nouns.

8. Write the sentence below using the correct verbs.
Mara and Pam plays the piano tomorrow.
Mara and Pam will play the piano tomorrow.

9. What type of verb tells about an action that is happening now?
present

10. Choose two answers that list correct present, past, future verbs.
● chase, chases, will chase
● add, added, will add
(C) handing, hands, is hand
(D) mover, moving, moved.

English Language Arts
34

Spectrum Test Prep Grade 1

34

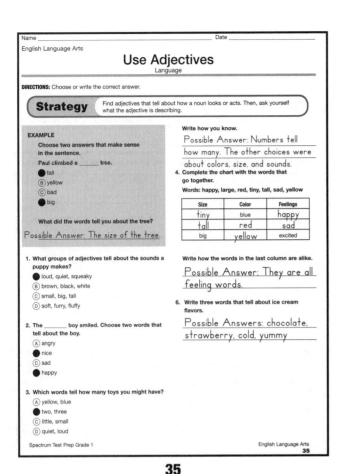

Use Adjectives
Language

DIRECTIONS: Choose or write the correct answer.

Strategy Find adjectives that tell about how a noun looks or acts. Then, ask yourself what the adjective is describing.

EXAMPLE

Choose two answers that make sense in the sentence.

Paul climbed a _____ tree.

● tall
Ⓑ yellow
Ⓒ bad
● big

What did the words tell you about the tree?

Possible Answer: The size of the tree.

1. What groups of adjectives tell about the sounds a puppy makes?
   ● loud, quiet, squeaky
   Ⓑ brown, black, white
   Ⓒ small, big, tall
   Ⓓ soft, furry, fluffy

2. The _____ boy smiled. Choose two words that tell about the boy.
   Ⓐ angry
   ● nice
   Ⓒ sad
   ● happy

3. Which words tell how many toys you might have?
   Ⓐ yellow, blue
   ● two, three
   Ⓒ little, small
   Ⓓ quiet, loud

Write how you know.

Possible Answer: Numbers tell how many. The other choices were about colors, size, and sounds.

4. Complete the chart with the words that go together.

Words: happy, large, red, tiny, tall, sad, yellow

Size	Color	Feelings
tiny	blue	happy
tall	red	sad
big	yellow	excited

Write how the words in the last column are alike.

Possible Answer: They are all feeling words.

6. Write three words that tell about ice cream flavors.

Possible Answers: chocolate, strawberry, cold, yummy

35

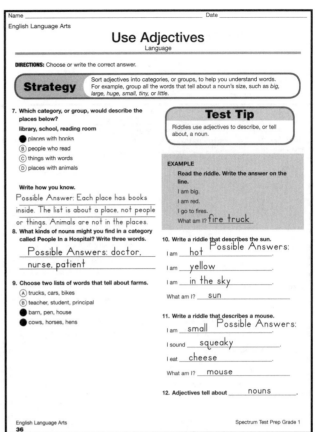

Use Adjectives
Language

DIRECTIONS: Choose or write the correct answer.

Strategy Sort adjectives into categories, or groups, to help you understand words. For example, group all the words that tell about a noun's size, such as *big, large, huge, small, tiny,* or *little.*

7. Which category, or group, would describe the places below?

   library, school, reading room
   ● places with books
   Ⓑ people who read
   Ⓒ things with words
   Ⓓ places with animals

Write how you know.

Possible Answer: Each place has books inside. The list is about a place, not people or things. Animals are not in the places.

8. What kinds of nouns might you find in a category called People In a Hospital? Write three words.

   Possible Answers: doctor, nurse, patient

9. Choose two lists of words that tell about farms.
   Ⓐ trucks, cars, bikes
   Ⓑ teacher, student, principal
   ● barn, pen, house
   ● cows, horses, hens

Test Tip

Riddles use adjectives to describe, or tell about, a noun.

EXAMPLE

Read the riddle. Write the answer on the line.

I am big.
I am red.
I go to fires.
What am I? fire truck

10. Write a riddle that describes the sun.
    I am __hot__ Possible Answers: .
    I am __yellow__ .
    I am __in the sky__ .
    What am I? __sun__

11. Write a riddle that describes a mouse.
    I am __small__ Possible Answers:
    I sound __squeaky__
    I eat __cheese__
    What am I? __mouse__

12. Adjectives tell about __nouns__ .

36

Use Articles and Prepositions
Language

DIRECTIONS: Choose or write the correct answer.

Strategy Identify prepositions by asking where a person, place, or thing is in a sentence. Or, find words that tell about time or when an action happens.

Test Tip Some words tell where a person, place, or thing is, such as *The glass is on the table* or *We sit in our chairs.* Other words tell about time, such as *We did not talk during class* or *I saw the movie on Monday.* Words that tell where or when are prepositions. Read each sentence and make sure the preposition makes sense. For example, a glass can sit *on* a table, not *over* or *above* a table.

1. The spider sits _____ the web.
   Ⓐ above
   Ⓑ over
   ● on
   Ⓓ after

Write how you know.

Possible Answer: The other words do not make sense. A spider cannot be above, over, or after a web.

2. Three apples are __under__ the tree.

Strategy Ask yourself if the nouns name a specific, or exact noun (the), or if they name any noun (a/an).

Test Tip An article is like an adjective because it tells about nouns. The word *a* tells if a noun is any person, place, or noun, like *a school.* The words *the* and *this* tells if a noun is about a specific, or exact, person, place or thing, like *the school* or *this school.*

EXAMPLES

We read a book in class every day.

Test Tip Look for clues in the sentence. The answer is *a*. You would not read the same book every day.

We read the book today in class.

Test Tip Look for clues in the sentence. The answer is *the*. The sentence tells about a specific, or exact, book.

3. My mom picked _____ blue flowers this morning.
   Ⓐ a
   ● the
   Ⓒ on
   Ⓓ in

Write how you know.

The sentence tells about specific flowers, so A is not correct. The other words tell where.

37

Use Articles and Prepositions
Language

DIRECTIONS: Choose or write the correct answer.

Strategy Make a list of prepositions that tell where (*on, under, over, above, in*) and prepositions that tell when (*during, before, after*). Use your list to find the best prepositions to use in a sentence.

Test Tip Remember that prepositions can also tell about time. Some prepositions tell where *and* when, such as *on* and *at*: *The book is on the shelf. The play is on Tuesday. We see the bird at the park. Lunch is at noon.*

4. We are going to see _____ movie everyone is talking about.
   Ⓐ a
   Ⓑ into
   ● the
   Ⓓ above

5. I saw blue birds __on__ a tree branch __on__ Monday.

6. Complete each sentence with a preposition.
   Yesterday I went for __a__ bike ride.
   I rode __in/to__ the park.
   I rode __over/across/onto__ the bridge.

Test Tip To tell about a specific noun, use the word *the*, like *I see the door to my classroom.* You can also use the words *this* and *that* for singular nouns. Use *these* or *those* for plural nouns.

7. Which words complete the sentence below?

   I saw _____ shoes we need for basketball _____ the store.
   Ⓐ a, over
   ● these, at
   Ⓒ this, on
   Ⓓ that, into

Test Tip For words that begin with a vowel sound, use the article *an*: *I ate an apple.*

8. Which article is correct in the sentence below?
   Dad made [a/an] egg for breakfast.
   an

9. Which word is incorrect in the sentence below?
   We saw a elephant at the zoo.
   Write the sentence so it is correct.
   a: We saw an elephant at the zoo.

38

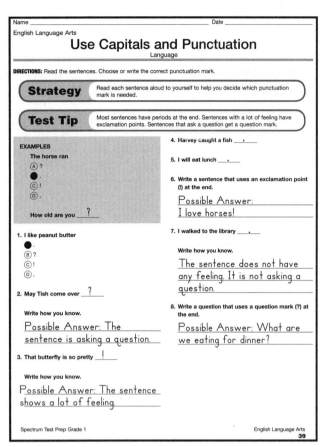

Page 39

Use Capitals and Punctuation
Language

DIRECTIONS: Read the sentences. Choose or write the correct punctuation mark.

Strategy Read each sentence aloud to yourself to help you decide which punctuation mark is needed.

Test Tip Most sentences have periods at the end. Sentences with a lot of feeling have exclamation points. Sentences that ask a question get a question mark.

EXAMPLES

The horse ran
- (A) ?
- ● .
- (C) !
- (D) .

How old are you __?__

1. I like peanut butter
- ● .
- (B) ?
- (C) !
- (D) .

2. May Tish come over __?__

Write how you know.
Possible Answer: The sentence is asking a question.

3. That butterfly is so pretty __!__

Write how you know.
Possible Answer: The sentence shows a lot of feeling.

4. Harvey caught a fish __.__

5. I will eat lunch __.__

6. Write a sentence that uses an exclamation point (!) at the end.
Possible Answer: I love horses!

7. I walked to the library __.__

Write how you know.
The sentence does not have any feeling. It is not asking a question.

8. Write a question that uses a question mark (?) at the end.
Possible Answer: What are we eating for dinner?

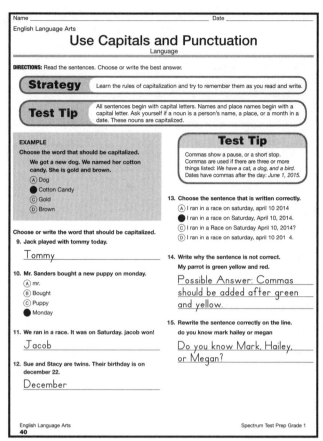

Page 40

Use Capitals and Punctuation
Language

DIRECTIONS: Read the sentences. Choose or write the best answer.

Strategy Learn the rules of capitalization and try to remember them as you read and write.

Test Tip All sentences begin with capital letters. Names and place names begin with a capital letter. Ask yourself if a noun is a person's name, a place, or a month in a date. These nouns are capitalized.

EXAMPLE

Choose the word that should be capitalized.
We got a new dog. We named her cotton candy. She is gold and brown.
- (A) Dog
- ● Cotton Candy
- (C) Gold
- (D) Brown

Choose or write the word that should be capitalized.
9. Jack played with tommy today.
Tommy

10. Mr. Sanders bought a new puppy on monday.
- (A) mr.
- (B) Bought
- (C) Puppy
- ● Monday

11. We ran in a race. It was on Saturday. jacob won!
Jacob

12. Sue and Stacy are twins. Their birthday is on december 22.
December

Test Tip
Commas show a pause, or a short stop. Commas are used if there are three or more things listed: We have a cat, a dog, and a bird. Dates have commas after the day: June 1, 2015.

13. Choose the sentence that is written correctly.
- (A) I ran in a race on saturday, april 10 2014
- ● I ran in a race on Saturday, April 10, 2014.
- (C) I ran in a Race on Saturday April 10, 2014?
- (D) I ran in a race on saturday, april 10 201 4.

14. Write why the sentence is not correct.
My parrot is green yellow and red.
Possible Answer: Commas should be added after green and yellow.

15. Rewrite the sentence correctly on the line.
do you know mark hailey or megan
Do you know Mark, Hailey, or Megan?

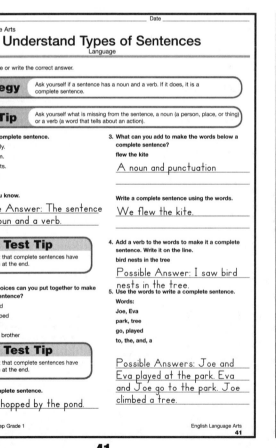

Page 41

Understand Types of Sentences
Language

DIRECTIONS: Choose or write the correct answer.

Strategy Ask yourself if a sentence has a noun and a verb. If it does, it is a complete sentence.

Test Tip Ask yourself what is missing from the sentence, a noun (a person, place, or thing) or a verb (a word that tells about an action).

1. Choose the complete sentence.
- (A) The butterfly.
- (B) Moon beam.
- ● The sun sets.
- (D) Ran home.

Write how you know.
Possible Answer: The sentence has a noun and a verb.

Test Tip
Don't forget that complete sentences have punctuation at the end.

2. Which two choices can you put together to make a complete sentence?
- ● by the pond
- ● A frog hopped
- (C) furry kitten
- (D) He and his brother

Test Tip
Don't forget that complete sentences have punctuation at the end.

Write the complete sentence.
A frog hopped by the pond.

3. What can you add to make the words below a complete sentence?
flew the kite
A noun and punctuation

Write a complete sentence using the words.
We flew the kite.

4. Add a verb to the words to make it a complete sentence. Write it on the line.
bird nests in the tree
Possible Answer: I saw bird nests in the tree.

5. Use the words to write a complete sentence.
Words:
Joe, Eva
park, tree
go, played
to, the, and, a
Possible Answers: Joe and Eva played at the park. Eva and Joe go to the park. Joe climbed a tree.

Page 42

Understand Types of Sentences
Language

DIRECTIONS: Choose or write the correct answer.

Strategy Categorize sentences as sentences that tell something or tell someone to do something (end with a period), ask something (end with a question mark), or show a lot of feeling (end with an exclamation point).

Test Tip Sentences can tell about something, ask a question, or tell someone to do something. Different types of sentences make stories more interesting. Look at the punctuation at the end to find out what kind of sentence it is. Sentences can also be joined together using the words and, but, or, and because.

EXAMPLES

Maria went to the store.
Did Juan see that movie?
Go home after school.

Ethan fed the dogs. They were hungry.
Ethan fed the dogs because they were hungry.

6. Join these sentences together. Write the new sentence on the line.
Ira ate a sandwich. He was hungry.
Possible Answer: Ira ate a sandwich because he was hungry.

7. Do you want to go to the beach? Do you want to go to the pool?
What kind of sentences are these? questions

Write how you know.
Possible Answer: A question asks something. It ends with a question mark.

Join these sentences together. Write the new sentence.
Possible Answer: Do you want to go to the beach, or do you want to go to the pool?

8. Choose two sentences that tell someone to do something.
- ● Study for the spelling test.
- (B) We met at the library.
- (C) I love that story.
- ● Sing me a song.

9. Join these sentences together. Write the new sentence.
Sue is sick. Jack gave her his cold.
Possible Answer: Sue is sick because Jack gave her his cold.

10. Read that book. Tell me about it.
What kind of sentences are these? commands

Write how you know.
Possible Answer: A command tells someone to do something.

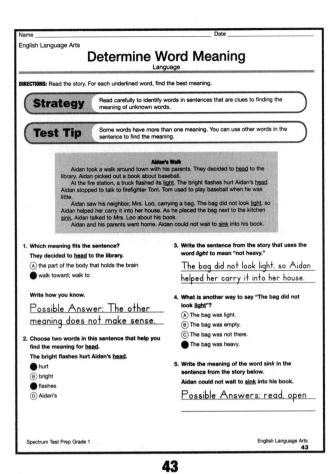

Page 43

Determine Word Meaning
Language

DIRECTIONS: Read the story. For each underlined word, find the best meaning.

Strategy — Read carefully to identify words in sentences that are clues to finding the meaning of unknown words.

Test Tip — Some words have more than one meaning. You can use other words in the sentence to find the meaning.

Aidan's Walk

Aidan took a walk around town with his parents. They decided to <u>head</u> to the library. Aidan picked out a book about baseball.

At the fire station, a truck flashed its <u>light</u>. The bright flashes hurt Aidan's <u>head</u>. Aidan stopped to talk to firefighter Tom. Tom used to play baseball when he was little.

Aidan saw his neighbor, Mrs. Loo, carrying a bag. The bag did not look <u>light</u>, so Aidan helped her carry it into her house. As he placed the bag next to the kitchen <u>sink</u>, Aidan talked to Mrs. Loo about his book.

Aidan and his parents went home. Aidan could not wait to <u>sink</u> into his book.

1. Which meaning fits the sentence?
They decided to <u>head</u> to the library.
Ⓐ the part of the body that holds the brain
● walk toward; walk to

Write how you know.
Possible Answer: The other meaning does not make sense.

2. Choose two words in this sentence that help you find the meaning for <u>head</u>.
The bright flashes hurt Aidan's <u>head</u>.
● hurt
Ⓑ bright
● flashes
Ⓓ Aidan's

3. Write the sentence from the story that uses the word *light* to mean "not heavy."
The bag did not look light, so Aidan helped her carry it into her house.

4. What is another way to say "The bag did not look <u>light</u>"?
Ⓐ The bag was light.
Ⓑ The bag was empty.
Ⓒ The bag was not there.
● The bag was heavy.

5. Write the meaning of the word *sink* in the sentence from the story below.
Aidan could not wait to <u>sink</u> into his book.
Possible Answers: read, open

43

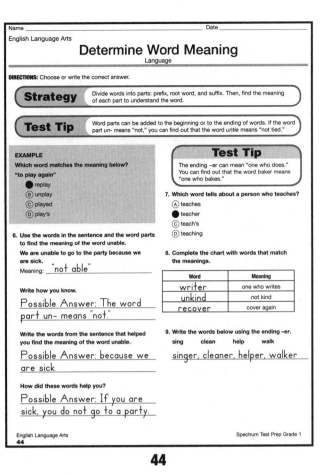

Page 44

Determine Word Meaning
Language

DIRECTIONS: Choose or write the correct answer.

Strategy — Divide words into parts: prefix, root word, and suffix. Then, find the meaning of each part to understand the word.

Test Tip — Word parts can be added to the beginning or to the ending of words. If the word part *un-* means "not," you can find out that the word *untie* means "not tied."

EXAMPLE
Which word matches the meaning below?
"to play again"
● replay
Ⓑ unplay
Ⓒ played
Ⓓ play's

6. Use the words in the sentence and the word parts to find the meaning of the word unable.
We are unable to go to the party because we are sick.
Meaning: **"not able"**

Write how you know.
Possible Answer: The word part un- means "not."

Write the words from the sentence that helped you find the meaning of the word unable.
Possible Answer: because we are sick

How did these words help you?
Possible Answer: If you are sick, you do not go to a party.

Test Tip — The ending *–er* can mean "one who does." You can find out that the word baker means "one who bakes."

7. Which word tells about a person who teaches?
Ⓐ teaches
● teacher
Ⓒ teach's
Ⓓ teaching

8. Complete the chart with words that match the meanings.

Word	Meaning
writer	one who writes
unkind	not kind
recover	cover again

9. Write the words below using the ending –er.
sing   clean   help   walk
singer, cleaner, helper, walker

44

Page 45

Write an Opinion
Writing

DIRECTIONS: An opinion paragraph tells how you feel about a topic. It gives reasons why you feel that way. Write an opinion paragraph for the school newspaper about your favorite season.

Your paragraph should have:
• A sentence that tells what your topic is.
• A sentence that tells how you feel about the topic.
• Some reasons for why you feel the way that you do.
• A sentence to end your paragraph.

Read the example paragraph to see how one student wrote an opinion paragraph about his favorite pet.

EXAMPLE
My favorite pet is a dog. I think dogs make the best pets. Dogs are friendly. They like to be close to you. They will wag their tail. Dogs protect you. They will bark if somebody comes to the house. I think dogs are the best pets.

Strategy — Use words such as *I think* or *I feel* to share your opinion Then, make sure you give reasons that tell why you think or feel the way you do.

Test Tip — Reread your paragraph. Did you use complete sentences? Did you capitalize dates and names of people? Did you use punctuation at the end of sentences?

Paragraphs should:
• introduce the topic
• state an opinion
• supply several reasons for the opinion
• provide a sense of closure
• capitalize dates and names of people
• use correct end punctuation

45

Page 46

Write an Opinion
Writing

DIRECTIONS: An opinion paragraph tells how you feel about a topic. It gives reasons why you feel that way. Write an opinion paragraph for a class book about your favorite food.

Your paragraph should have:
• A sentence that tells what your topic is.
• A sentence that tells how you feel about the topic.
• Some reasons for why you feel the way that you do.
• A sentence to end your paragraph.

Read the example paragraph to see how one student wrote an opinion paragraph about her favorite holiday.

EXAMPLE
My favorite holiday is Halloween. Halloween is on October 31 every year. I think Halloween is the most fun holiday of all. I like to get dressed up on Halloween. My favorite costume is a princess. I also like to go trick–or–treating on Halloween. I think it is fun to see everyone in their costumes. I think Halloween is the best holiday.

Test Tip — Reread your paragraph. Are all of your sentences about your favorite food? Make sure you focus only on the topic.

Paragraphs should:
• introduce the topic
• state an opinion
• supply several reasons for the opinion
• provide a sense of closure
• capitalize dates and names of people
• use correct end punctuation

46

Write an Informative Paragraph
Writing

DIRECTIONS: An informative paragraph gives facts about a topic. Use what you already know and the facts below to write an informative paragraph about healthy foods.

Your paragraph should have:
• A topic sentence
• Some facts about the topic
• A sentence to end your paragraph

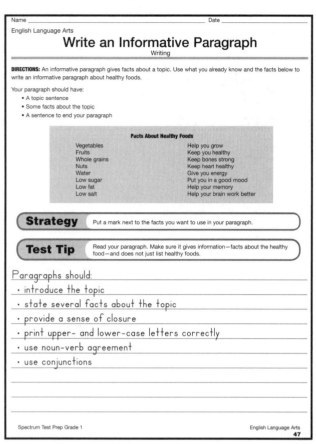

Facts About Healthy Foods

Vegetables	Help you grow
Fruits	Keep you healthy
Whole grains	Keep bones strong
Nuts	Keep heart healthy
Water	Give you energy
Low sugar	Put you in a good mood
Low fat	Help your memory
Low salt	Help your brain work better

Strategy Put a mark next to the facts you want to use in your paragraph.

Test Tip Read your paragraph. Make sure it gives information—facts about the healthy food—and does not just list healthy foods.

Paragraphs should:
· introduce the topic
· state several facts about the topic
· provide a sense of closure
· print upper- and lower-case letters correctly
· use noun-verb agreement
· use conjunctions

Write an Explanatory Paragraph
Writing

DIRECTIONS: An explanatory paragraph gives directions for doing something. Choose a topic from the list. Write an explanatory paragraph telling how to do it.

Your paragraph should have:
• A topic sentence
• Clear steps to follow
• A sentence to end your paragraph

Topics

How to make a sandwich (you pick what kind!)	How to play a game (you pick the game!)
How to make a bed	How to walk to school
How to wash a dog	How to brush your teeth

Strategy After you choose a topic, make a list of the steps. Number the steps to keep track of what comes first, next, and last.

Test Tip Use words like *first, next, then,* and *finally* to show the order of steps to follow.

Paragraphs should:
· introduce the topic
· provide clear steps to follow
· provide a sense of closure
· print upper- and lower-case letters correctly
· use noun-verb agreement
· use conjunctions

Write a Narrative
Writing

Test Tip Look back at your graphic organizer and reread all of the details about your favorite place. Which details are the most important? Use these details in your narrative. Before writing, read the directions one more time to make sure you include everything.

Narratives should:
· Recount two or more sequenced events
· Include details of what happened
· Use temporal words
· Provide a sense of closure
· Use adjectives

Strategy Review

In this section, you will review the strategies you learned and apply them to practice the skills.

Strategy Use details in the story to make a picture in your mind as you read. Use details to show your understanding.

When you read a story, think about the details as you read. Make connections to things you already know about a topic. Make connections to another story you read. Use these details and connections to help you understand the story better.

Read the story carefully. Then, answer the questions using details from the story.

> Mr. Weinstein took his children to the zoo. Austin wanted to see the flamingoes. He liked how they stood on one leg. Ethan wanted to see the giraffes. Giraffes were Ethan's favorite animal. Mr. Weinstein wanted to see the bears. He liked how they played together.

First, read the story. Think about what you know about zoos.

Next, make a connection. When you go to a zoo, what animals do you like to visit? Why do you like to visit that animal? Compare characters to make more connections. How are they alike? How are they different?

Finally, read the questions that go with the story. Reread the story if you need to. Look for key words in the question and then, find the answers in the story.

1. **What animal did Austin want to visit?**
   Ⓐ giraffe
   Ⓑ lion
   Ⓒ bear
   ● flamingo

> Next, he visited the giraffes. Their long necks reached into the treetops. They were having a tasty breakfast of oak leaves. Finally, the zookeeper went by the bear habitat. The baby bears were rolling around together in the dirt. They looked like they were having a great time.

2. **Why did Mr. Weinstein want to go see the bears?**
   Ⓐ He liked how they stood on one leg.
   ● He liked how they played together.
   Ⓒ They were his favorite animal.
   Ⓓ He liked to watch them eat.

Read the next story about a zoo. Think about how it is the same as the story you just read. Think about how it is different.

> It was a bright, warm morning. The zookeeper was making his rounds. First, he stopped to see the flamingoes. He watched them clean their pink feathers. He gave them some shrimp for breakfast.

3. **What words helped you make a picture in your mind?**

   Possible Answer: bright, warm morning, pink feathers, long necks reached into the treetops, rolling around in the dirt.

4. **Write how the two stories are alike.**

   Possible Answer: Both stories are about visiting animals at a zoo.

Name _____ Date _____
English Language Arts

Strategy Review

Strategy Look carefully at pictures to help you understand words better.

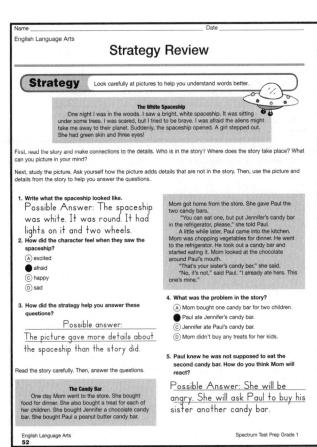

The White Spaceship
One night I was in the woods. I saw a bright, white spaceship. It was sitting under some trees. I was scared, but I tried to be brave. I was afraid the aliens might take me away to their planet. Suddenly, the spaceship opened. A girl stepped out. She had green skin and three eyes!

First, read the story and make connections to the details. Who is in the story? Where does the story take place? What can you picture in your mind?

Next, study the picture. Ask yourself how the picture adds details that are not in the story. Then, use the picture and details from the story to help you answer the questions.

1. Write what the spaceship looked like.

Possible Answer: The spaceship was white. It was round. It had lights on it and two wheels.

2. How did the character feel when they saw the spaceship?
Ⓐ excited
● afraid
Ⓒ happy
Ⓓ sad

3. How did the strategy help you answer these questions?

Possible answer: The picture gave more details about the spaceship than the story did.

Read the story carefully. Then, answer the questions.

The Candy Bar
One day Mom went to the store. She bought food for dinner. She also bought a treat for each of her children. She bought Jennifer a chocolate candy bar. She bought Paul a peanut butter candy bar.

Mom got home from the store. She gave Paul the two candy bars.
"You can eat one, but put Jennifer's candy bar in the refrigerator, please," she told Paul.
A little while later, Paul came into the kitchen. Mom was chopping vegetables for dinner. He went to the refrigerator. He took out a candy bar and started eating it. Mom looked at the chocolate around Paul's mouth.
"That's your sister's candy bar," she said.
"No, it's not," said Paul. "I already ate hers. This one's mine."

4. What was the problem in the story?
Ⓐ Mom bought one candy bar for two children.
● Paul ate Jennifer's candy bar.
Ⓒ Jennifer ate Paul's candy bar.
Ⓓ Mom didn't buy any treats for her kids.

5. Paul knew he was not supposed to eat the second candy bar. How do you think Mom will react?

Possible Answer: She will be angry. She will ask Paul to buy his sister another candy bar.

52

Name _____ Date _____
English Language Arts

Strategy Review

Strategy Plan your writing using a graphic organizer.

Julio wanted to write a paragraph that tells how pigs and ducks are different and alike. He started by planning his paragraph. He used a graphic organizer called a Venn diagram to organize the information he wanted to include.

First, Julio wrote information that is true about pigs, but not about ducks.

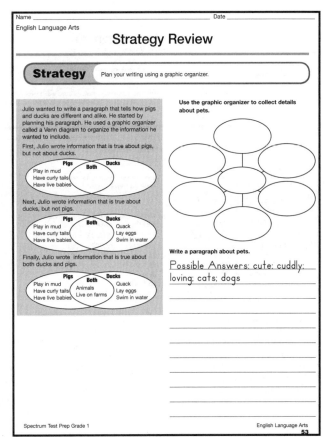

Use the graphic organizer to collect details about pets.

Next, Julio wrote information that is true about ducks, but not pigs.

Finally, Julio wrote information that is true about both ducks and pigs.

Write a paragraph about pets.

Possible Answers: cute; cuddly; loving; cats; dogs

53

Name _____ Date _____
English Language Arts

Strategy Review

Strategy Revise to make sure your writing is clear and makes sense. Then, edit to fix errors.

After you write your first draft, you should reread it. Read the story aloud to yourself to make sure it makes sense. Look for places where the reader might have trouble understanding what you want to say. Look for words that need capitals. Look for places that need punctuation marks. Finally, look for words that might be spelled wrong.

Once upon a time, there was a little girl name hannah. She lived with her mother and father in the woods she was very nice. All of the animals played with her. They went to the village one day. They bought a cake. Then, they went home and had a party.

First, read the story to make sure it makes sense.
There is a sentence that is not very clear: "They went to the village one day." Does this mean the family or the animals? Rewrite the sentence to make it clear. "Hannah and her parents went to the village one day."

Next, look for words that need capitals.
Hannah is a name, so it should have a capital letter.

Then, look for places that need punctuation marks.
There is a run-on sentence: "She lived with her mother and father in the woods she was very nice." Put a period after woods. Use a capital letter for she.

Finally, look for spelling mistakes.
"Once upon a time, there was a little girl name Hannah." There should be a d at the end of *name*.

1. Find the mistakes in this sentence. Then, write the sentence correctly on the lines.
James and marta went shoping at the mall?

Answer: James and Marta went shopping at the mall.

2. Find the mistakes in this sentence. Then, write the sentence correctly on the lines.
Do you like chocolate or vanilla? Chocolates my favrit.

Answer: Do you like chocolate or vanilla? Chocolate's my favorite.

54

Name _____ Date _____
Math

Solve Problems: Add Within 20
Operations and Algebraic Thinking

DIRECTIONS: Read the problems. Then, answer the questions.

EXAMPLE
Mia has 6 apples. She buys 2 more apples. Write numbers to complete the number sentence to find out how many apples Mia has all together.

☐ _____ = _____
6 + 2 = 8
Mia has 8 apples all together.

Strategy When using addition, ask yourself what you are adding and how many of each.

Test Tip Read carefully to understand what the problem asks you to do. Problems may ask you to put together numbers, add numbers, or compare numbers.

1. Kim and Lisa counted birds. Kim counted 5 birds and Lisa counted 8 birds. Write a number sentence that shows how many birds they counted in all.

5 + 8 = 13, or 8 + 5 = 13

2. Carlos bought a notebook at the school store for 10¢. He also bought a pencil for 5¢. How much did Carlos spend in all? Use words, numbers, or pictures to show how you found your answer.

15¢; numbers: 10 + 5 = 15, or 5 + 10 = 15; words: I added 10¢ and 5¢ to find how much Carlos spent; picture: Draw 10 objects plus 5 more objects to show a total of 15 objects.

3. David read 9 pages in his book on Monday. On Tuesday, he read 2 more pages than he did on Monday. How many pages did David read on Tuesday?

11 pages; 9 + 2 = 11

Write a sentence that tells how you found your answer.

Possible answer: On Monday, David read 9 pages. On Tuesday he read 2 more pages than on Monday, so he read 9 plus 2 equals 11 pages.

4. Six horses were eating grass in a field. More horses ran into the field. Now there are 14 horses in the field. Which number sentence shows how many horses ran into the field?
● 6 + 8 = 14
Ⓑ 14 + 6 = 20
Ⓒ 6 + 6 = 12
Ⓓ 7 + 7 = 14

Write how you found the answer.

Possible answer: There were 6 horses. I know that to add to 14, there were 8 more horses.

56

Solve Problems: Add Within 20
Operations and Algebraic Thinking

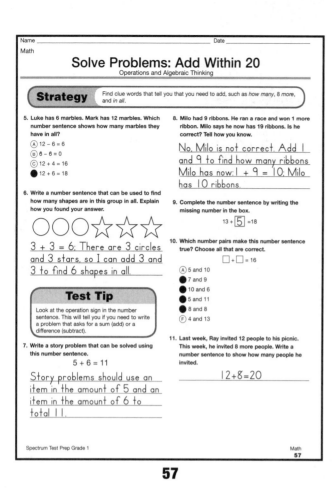

Strategy Find clue words that tell you that you need to add, such as *how many*, *8 more*, and *in all*.

5. Luke has 6 marbles. Mark has 12 marbles. Which number sentence shows how many marbles they have in all?
- Ⓐ 12 − 6 = 6
- Ⓑ 6 − 6 = 0
- Ⓒ 12 + 4 = 16
- ● 12 + 6 = 18

6. Write a number sentence that can be used to find how many shapes are in this group in all. Explain how you found your answer.

○○○☆☆☆

3 + 3 = 6; There are 3 circles and 3 stars, so I can add 3 and 3 to find 6 shapes in all.

Test Tip
Look at the operation sign in the number sentence. This will tell you if you need to write a problem that asks for a sum (add) or a difference (subtract).

7. Write a story problem that can be solved using this number sentence.
5 + 6 = 11
Story problems should use an item in the amount of 5 and an item in the amount of 6 to total 11.

8. Milo had 9 ribbons. He ran a race and won 1 more ribbon. Milo says he now has 19 ribbons. Is he correct? Tell how you know.
No, Milo is not correct. Add 1 and 9 to find how many ribbons Milo has now: 1 + 9 = 10; Milo has 10 ribbons.

9. Complete the number sentence by writing the missing number in the box.
13 + ☐5 = 18

10. Which number pairs make this number sentence true? Choose all that are correct.
☐ + ☐ = 16
- Ⓐ 5 and 10
- ● 7 and 9
- ● 10 and 6
- ● 5 and 11
- ● 8 and 8
- Ⓕ 4 and 13

11. Last week, Ray invited 12 people to his picnic. This week, he invited 8 more people. Write a number sentence to show how many people he invited.
12 + 8 = 20

Math 57

57

Solve Problems: Subtract Within 20
Operations and Algebraic Thinking

DIRECTIONS: Choose the best answer.

Strategy Show your answer in different ways: drawings, number sentences, and word problems.

Test Tip Draw objects to help you write a number sentence.

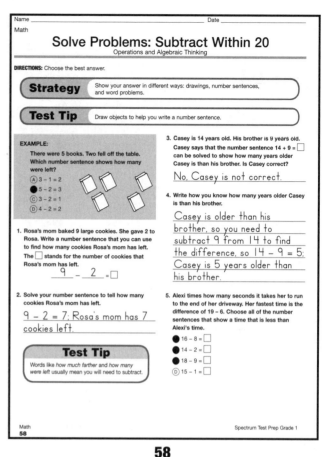

EXAMPLE:
There were 5 books. Two fell off the table. Which number sentence shows how many were left?
- Ⓐ 3 − 1 = 2
- ● 5 − 2 = 3
- Ⓒ 3 − 2 = 1
- Ⓓ 4 − 2 = 2

1. Rosa's mom baked 9 large cookies. She gave 2 to Rosa. Write a number sentence that you can use to find how many cookies Rosa's mom has left. The ☐ stands for the number of cookies that Rosa's mom has left.
9 − 2 = ☐

2. Solve your number sentence to tell how many cookies Rosa's mom has left.
9 − 2 = 7; Rosa's mom has 7 cookies left.

Test Tip
Words like *how much farther* and *how many were left* usually mean you will need to subtract.

3. Casey is 14 years old. His brother is 9 years old. Casey says that the number sentence 14 + 9 = ☐ can be solved to show how many years older Casey is than his brother. Is Casey correct?
No, Casey is not correct.

4. Write how you know how many years older Casey is than his brother.
Casey is older than his brother, so you need to subtract 9 from 14 to find the difference, so 14 − 9 = 5; Casey is 5 years older than his brother.

5. Alexi times how many seconds it takes her to run to the end of her driveway. Her fastest time is the difference of 19 − 6. Choose all of the number sentences that show a time that is less than Alexi's time.
- ● 16 − 8 = ☐
- ● 14 − 2 = ☐
- ● 18 − 9 = ☐
- Ⓓ 15 − 1 = ☐

58

Solve Problems: Subtract Within 20
Operations and Algebraic Thinking

6. Kyle read his book for 15 minutes. Kevin read his book for 10 minutes. Aram read his book for 14 minutes. Felipe read his book for 9 minutes. Who read his book for 17 minutes − 3 minutes? Tell how you know.
The difference of 17 − 3 is 14; Aram read his book for 14 minutes.

7. Jake has 15 car stickers. He gave his friend 9 of the stickers. How many car stickers does Jake have now? Draw a picture and write a number sentence to show how you found your answer.
Possible Answer: a picture of 15 squares (stickers) and 9 of them crossed out to show 6 left; 15 − 9 = 6

8. Lia gave her friends some fruit juice and had 3 glasses left. How many glasses of fruit juice did Lia give to her friends? Use numbers or pictures to show your work.

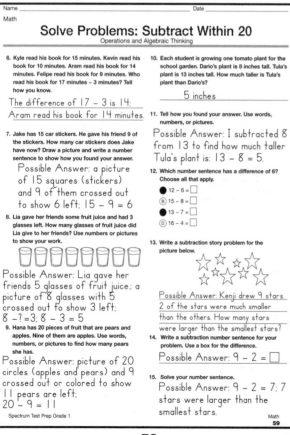

Possible Answer: Lia gave her friends 5 glasses of fruit juice.: a picture of 8 glasses with 5 crossed out to show 3 left; 8 − ? = 3; 8 − 3 = 5

9. Hana has 20 pieces of fruit that are pears and apples. Nine of them are apples. Use words, numbers, or pictures to find how many pears she has.
Possible Answer: picture of 20 circles (apples and pears) and 9 crossed out or colored to show 11 pears are left; 20 − 9 = 11

10. Each student is growing one tomato plant for the school garden. Dario's plant is 8 inches tall. Tula's plant is 13 inches tall. How much taller is Tula's plant than Dario's?
5 inches

11. Tell how you found your answer. Use words, numbers, or pictures.
Possible Answer: I subtracted 8 from 13 to find how much taller Tula's plant is: 13 − 8 = 5.

12. Which number sentence has a difference of 6? Choose all that apply.
- ● 12 − 6 = ☐
- Ⓑ 15 − 8 = ☐
- ● 13 − 7 = ☐
- Ⓓ 16 − 4 = ☐

13. Write a subtraction story problem for the picture below.
☆☆☆ ☆☆ ☆☆ ☆☆
Possible Answer: Kenji drew 9 stars. 2 of the stars were much smaller than the others. How many stars were larger than the smallest stars?

14. Write a subtraction number sentence for your problem. Use a box for the difference.
Possible Answer: 9 − 2 = ☐

15. Solve your number sentence.
Possible Answer: 9 − 2 = 7; 7 stars were larger than the smallest stars.

Math 59

59

Solve Problems: Add 3 Whole Numbers
Operations and Algebraic Thinking

DIRECTIONS: Answer the questions.

Strategy Add three numbers in different ways. Add the numbers in order. Or make a ten first and then, add the other number.

EXAMPLE
Liza has some fruit. She has 3 apples, 4 pears, and 6 oranges.
Write a number sentence you can use to find how many pieces of fruit Liza has in all. The ☐ represents the unknown number.
3 + 4 + 6 = ☐ pieces of fruit
Show one way to add the three numbers and tell how many pieces of fruit Liza has in all.
I can add 4 plus 6 and get 10, and add on 3 more to make 13. Liza has 13 pieces of fruit.

1. Jake scored 3 goals, Trey scored 5 goals, and Pedro scored 7 goals. How many goals did the boys score in all?
- Ⓐ 8
- Ⓑ 10
- Ⓒ 12
- ● 15

2. Choose the number sentences that have a sum of 18.
- Ⓐ 6 + 3 + 8 = ☐
- ● 7 + 8 + 3 = ☐
- ● 9 + 6 + 3 = ☐
- ● 8 + 2 + 8 = ☐

3. Write an addition number sentence for the picture below. Use a ☐ for the total number of birds.
2 + 3 + 5 = ☐

4. Complete your number sentence to tell how many birds in all.
2 + 3 + 5 = 10; 10 birds in all

5. 10 + 5 is the same as _____.
- Ⓐ 4 + 7 + 6
- Ⓑ 6 + 2 + 8
- Ⓒ 3 + 3 + 7
- ● 5 + 5 + 5

6. Mrs. Cruz ran 4 miles yesterday and 2 miles today. She will run 4 miles tomorrow. How many miles will Mrs. Cruz run in all? Use numbers and a picture to show how you know.
4 + 2 + 4 = 10; or a number line 0 to 10, showing jumps of 4 + 2 + 4 and ending at 10

60

Solve Problems: Add 3 Whole Numbers
Operations and Algebraic Thinking

Strategy When writing number sentences, first, write the numbers you have from the problem. Then, write the operation sign needed. Finally, solve for the missing number.

7. Alonzo raked 3 + 6 + 7 bags of leaves. Rachel raked the same number of bags of leaves as Alonzo. Which two number sentences show the number of bags of leaves that Rachel raked in all?

(A) ☐ = 5 + 5 + 3
● ☐ = 3 + 10 + 3
● ☐ = 9 + 7 + 0
(D) ☐ = 7 + 5 + 3

8. Rita drew the picture below.

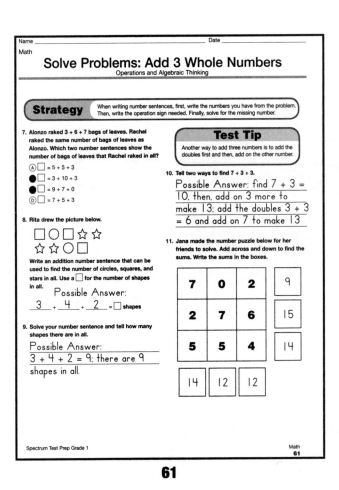

☐ ○ ☐ ☆ ☆
☆ ☆ ○ ☐

Write an addition number sentence that can be used to find the number of circles, squares, and stars in all. Use a ☐ for the number of shapes in all.

Possible Answer:
3 + 4 + 2 = ☐ shapes

9. Solve your number sentence and tell how many shapes there are in all.

Possible Answer:
3 + 4 + 2 = 9; there are 9 shapes in all.

Test Tip
Another way to add three numbers is to add the doubles first and then, add on the other number.

10. Tell two ways to find 7 + 3 + 3.

Possible Answer: find 7 + 3 = 10, then, add on 3 more to make 13; add the doubles 3 + 3 = 6 and add on 7 to make 13

11. Jana made the number puzzle below for her friends to solve. Add across and down to find the sums. Write the sums in the boxes.

7	0	2	9
2	7	6	15
5	5	4	14

14	12	12

Use Properties of Operations: Add
Operations and Algebraic Thinking

DIRECTIONS: Answer the questions.

Strategy Write addition problems in a different order to find the sum and check your answer: 3 + 9 = 12, 9 + 3 = 12, 12 = 9 + 3.

Test Tip If you add numbers together in any order, you will get the same sum.

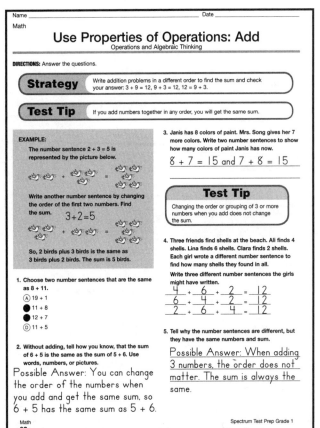

EXAMPLE:
The number sentence 2 + 3 = 5 is represented by the picture below.

Write another number sentence by changing the order of the first two numbers. Find the sum. 3 + 2 = 5

So, 2 birds plus 3 birds is the same as 3 birds plus 2 birds. The sum is 5 birds.

1. Choose two number sentences that are the same as 8 + 11.

(A) 19 + 1
● 11 + 8
● 12 + 7
(D) 11 + 5

2. Without adding, tell how you know, that the sum of 6 + 5 is the same as the sum of 5 + 6. Use words, numbers, or pictures.

Possible Answer: You can change the order of the numbers when you add and get the same sum, so 6 + 5 has the same sum as 5 + 6.

3. Janis has 8 colors of paint. Mrs. Song gives her 7 more colors. Write two number sentences to show how many colors of paint Janis has now.

8 + 7 = 15 and 7 + 8 = 15

Test Tip
Changing the order or grouping of 3 or more numbers when you add does not change the sum.

4. Three friends find shells at the beach. Ali finds 4 shells. Lina finds 6 shells. Clara finds 2 shells. Each girl wrote a different number sentence to find how many shells they found in all.

Write three different number sentences the girls might have written.

4 + 6 + 2 = 12
6 + 4 + 2 = 12
2 + 6 + 4 = 12

5. Tell why the number sentences are different, but they have the same numbers and sum.

Possible Answer: When adding 3 numbers, the order does not matter. The sum is always the same.

Use Properties of Operations: Add
Operations and Algebraic Thinking

Strategy It doesn't matter which order you write addition number sentences in, but check the story problem to make sure you have the right numbers.

6. Dora and Emma are playing a game. Dora scores 5 points and then, she scores 3 more points. Emma scores 3 points and then, she scores 5 more points. Which girl has the most points in all? Tell how you know.

They have the same number of points; 5 + 3 is the same as 3 + 5. The sum is 8.

Test Tip
Make a ten first, and then, add the other number.

7. Tell how to add 8 + 2 + 8.

Possible Answer: You can add 8 + 2 to make 10, and then, add 10 + 8 to get 18; or you can add the 8 + 8 to get 16 and add 16 + 2 to get 18.

8. Show how you know by drawing a picture.

Possible Answer:
picture showing 8 objects + 2 objects + 8 objects = 18 objects; or 8 objects + 8 objects + 2 objects = 18 objects.

9. Look at the picture below. Write two addition number sentences that go with the picture.

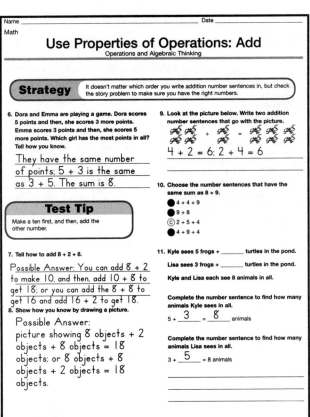

4 + 2 = 6; 2 + 4 = 6

10. Choose the number sentences that have the same sum as 8 + 9.

● 4 + 4 + 9
● 9 + 8
(C) 2 + 5 + 4
● 4 + 9 + 4

11. Kyle sees 5 frogs + _____ turtles in the pond.

Lisa sees 3 frogs + _____ turtles in the pond.

Kyle and Lisa each see 8 animals in all.

Complete the number sentence to find how many animals Kyle sees in all.

5 + 3 = 8 animals

Complete the number sentence to find how many animals Lisa sees in all.

3 + 5 = 8 animals

Find the Unknown Addend to Subtract
Operations and Algebraic Thinking

DIRECTIONS: Answer the questions.

Strategy Use addition facts to solve subtraction problems. For example, to find the answer to 15 – 3 = ☐, use 3 + 12 = 15.

EXAMPLE
Find 11 – 8 = ☐.
Use a known addition fact to find the difference.
Think: 8 and what number makes 11?
8 + ? = 11
8 + 3 = 11
So, 11 – 8 = 3

Test Tip
If you know the addition fact, you can use it to find the difference.

1. What addition fact can be used to find the difference: 14 – 6 = ☐?

(A) 14 + 6 = 20
(B) 5 + 8 = 14
(C) 6 + 6 = 12
● 8 + 6 = 14

2. Tell how Jane can use an addition fact to find the difference of 10 – 6.

Possible Answer: Jane can ask, 6 and what number makes 10? She knows that 6 and 4 make 10, so 10 – 6 = 4.

Test Tip
When you subtract 9 or 10 from a number, add either 1 or 2 to the number to make 10. Then, add on the other number for the final sum.

3. Find 14 – 9.
5

4. Explain how you found the answer.
Possible Answer: I used an addition fact and found what number plus 9 makes 14; 9 + 5 = 14, so 14 – 9 = 5; or, I added 1 to 9 to make 10. Then, I needed 4 more to make 14, so 1 + 4 = 5.

5. Which differences can be found by using the addition fact 4 + 9?

● 13 – 9 = 4
(B) 9 – 5 = 4
(C) 9 – 4 = 5
● 13 – 4 = 9

6. What addition fact can help you subtract 15 – 6 and 15 – 9. Why?

Possible Answer: 6 + 9 = 15; so 15 – 6 = 9 and 15 – 9 = 6

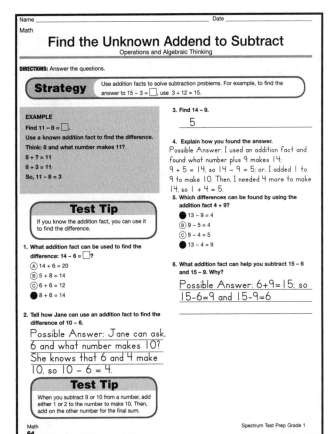

Find the Unknown Addend to Subtract
Operations and Algebraic Thinking

Strategy Use addition and subtraction facts to solve problems. For example, $16 - 5 = 11$ is related to $16 - 11 = 5$ and $11 + 5 = 16$ is the same as $5 + 11 = 16$.

7. Complete the addition fact below.

$7 + 6 = 13$

8. Write two subtraction facts to match the addition fact.

$13 - 7 = 6$

$13 - 6 = 7$

9. Use the numbers 7, 9, and 16. Write two addition facts and two related subtraction facts.

$7 + 9 = 16$

$9 + 7 = 16$

$16 - 7 = 9$

$16 - 9 = 7$

DIRECTIONS: Write a number sentence. Solve it.

10. Alberto puts 12 pennies in his bank. He gets 5 more pennies and puts them in his bank. How many pennies are in Alberto's bank now?

$12 + 5 = 17$ pennies

11. There are 17 pennies in Alberto's bank. He gives 5 pennies to his brother. How many pennies are in Alberto's bank now?

$17 - 5 = 12$ pennies

12. Write an addition word problem and a related subtraction word problem using the numbers 3, 6, and 9.

Possible Answer: addition problem: Kayla has 6 fish in a bowl. She puts 3 more fish in the bowl. How many fish in all are now in the bowl? Subtraction story: Kayla has 9 fish in a bowl. She puts 3 of the fish in a new bowl. How many fish are in the first bowl?

13. Write number sentences for your problems.

Possible Answer: $6 + 3 = 9$; $9 - 3 = 6$

14. Choose which facts are related to $9 + 8 = 17$.

● $8 + 9 = 17$
● $17 - 8 = 9$
ⓒ $17 + 8 = 25$
● $17 - 9 = 8$

65

Use Counting Strategies: Add and Subtract
Operations and Algebraic Thinking

DIRECTIONS: Answer the questions.

Strategy Relate addition and subtraction to counting. Count all objects and then, count on (add) or count back (subtract).

EXAMPLE

Jake wants to draw 2 more bubbles in the picture. How many bubbles will there be if Jake draws two more bubbles? Tell how you know.

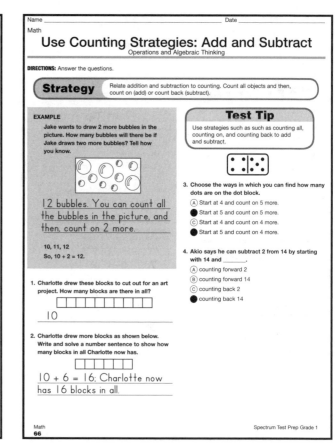

12 bubbles. You can count all the bubbles in the picture, and then, count on 2 more.

10, 11, 12
So, $10 + 2 = 12$.

1. Charlotte drew these blocks to cut out for an art project. How many blocks are there in all?

10

2. Charlotte drew more blocks as shown below. Write and solve a number sentence to show how many blocks in all Charlotte now has.

$10 + 6 = 16$; Charlotte now has 16 blocks in all.

Test Tip

Use strategies such as such as counting all, counting on, and counting back to add and subtract.

3. Choose the ways in which you can find how many dots are on the dot block.

Ⓐ Start at 4 and count on 5 more.
● Start at 5 and count on 5 more.
ⓒ Start at 4 and count on 4 more.
Ⓐ Start at 5 and count on 4 more.

4. Akio says he can subtract 2 from 14 by starting with 14 and _____.

Ⓐ counting forward 2
Ⓑ counting forward 14
ⓒ counting back 2
● counting back 14

66

Use Counting Strategies: Add and Subtract
Operations and Algebraic Thinking

Strategy Write number lines, number sentences, or count out loud to solve problems.

Test Tip Re-read each problem and answer to be sure you have followed the directions.

5. Which picture makes this number sentence true?

5 apples + ▢ apples = 9 apples

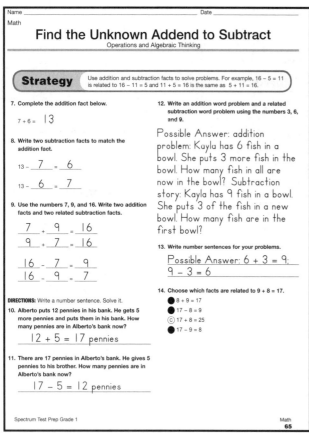

6. Write a number to finish each sentence.

a. 1 more than 47 is 48.

b. 2 less than 23 is 21.

c. 1 less than 60 is 59.

d. 2 more than 35 is 37.

7. Daria solves a math problem by counting out loud. She counts. "5, 6, 7, 8, 9, 10, 11, 12."
Write a number sentence that Daria could be solving. Possible Answer:

$5 + 7 = 12$

8. Leo uses a number line to solve a math problem. He starts at number 17 and counts back. He stops at number 9. Write a number sentence with its answer to show the problem that Leo is solving. Possible Answer:

$17 - 9 = 8$

9. Lydia starts at a number and counts up to 19. Which number sentences can Lydia write to show her work?

Ⓐ $7 + 6 = ▢$
● $10 + 9 = ▢$
● $12 + 7 = ▢$
● $5 + 14 = ▢$

10. Write count up or count back for each number sentence.

$9 + 9 = ▢$ count up

$14 - 3 = ▢$ count back

$6 + 6 = ▢$ count up

$9 - 9 = ▢$ count back

67

Solve Problems: Use Addition and Subtraction Strategies
Operations and Algebraic Thinking

DIRECTIONS: Answer the questions.

Strategy As you read each problem, choose a strategy: counting all, counting on, or counting back to add and subtract.

EXAMPLE

Tara wants to solve this problem: Two bunnies are sitting in the yard. Five more bunnies hop into the yard. How many bunnies are in the yard now?

Tara can count on to find how many bunnies.

Answer: Start at 2 and count on 5 more, "3, 4, 5, 6, 7."
$2 + 5 = 7$
There are 7 bunnies in the yard now.

1. Which two pairs are equal?

● $3 + 4$ and $5 + 2$
Ⓑ $16 - 8$ and $9 + 9$
● $6 + 7$ and $15 - 2$
Ⓓ $2 + 10$ and $8 + 3$

2. Fill in each box with one of the numbers below to complete each number sentence. Use each number only once. You will not use one number.

2	4	6	7	9

a. $9 + \boxed{7} = 16$

b. $10 - 1 = \boxed{9}$

c. $\boxed{4} + 8 = 12$

d. $\boxed{6} - 3 = 3$

3. Write three different number sentences using only the numbers in the box below. Use ◯ to fill in the operation sign. Possible Answers:

4	5	6	9	11	10	15

$4 ⊕ 5 = 9$

$5 ⊕ 6 = 11$

$15 ⊖ 9 = 6$

4. Marco's model plane is 6 inches long. Kyle's model plane is 14 inches long. How much longer is Kyle's model plane than Marco's?

8 inches

Write how you know.

Possible Answers: I started with 6 and counted on 8 to get to 14; or I wrote a number sentence and solved it: $14 - 6 = 8$.

68

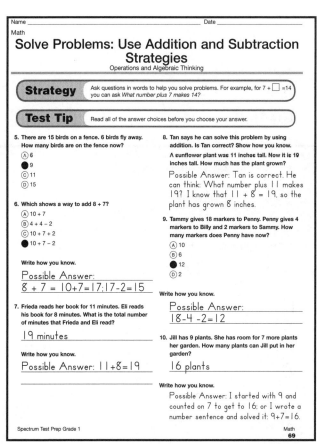

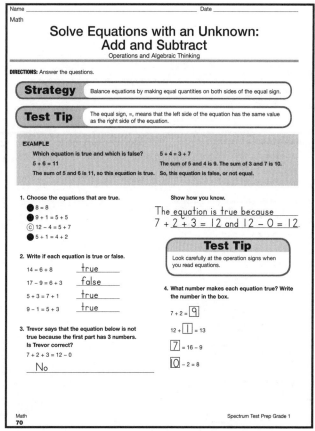

Page 69

Name _____ Date _____
Math

Solve Problems: Use Addition and Subtraction Strategies
Operations and Algebraic Thinking

Strategy Ask questions in words to help you solve problems. For example, for 7 + ☐ =14 you can ask *What number plus 7 makes 14?*

Test Tip Read all of the answer choices before you choose your answer.

5. There are 15 birds on a fence. 6 birds fly away. How many birds are on the fence now?
   - (A) 6
   - ● 9
   - (C) 11
   - (D) 15

6. Which shows a way to add 8 + 7?
   - (A) 10 + 7
   - (B) 4 + 4 − 2
   - (C) 10 + 7 + 2
   - ● 10 + 7 − 2

Write how you know.

Possible Answer:
8 + 7 = 10+7=17; 17−2=15

7. Frieda reads her book for 11 minutes. Eli reads his book for 8 minutes. What is the total number of minutes that Frieda and Eli read?

19 minutes

Write how you know.

Possible Answer: 11+8=19

8. Tan says he can solve this problem by using addition. Is Tan correct? Show how you know.

A sunflower plant was 11 inches tall. Now it is 19 inches tall. How much has the plant grown?

Possible Answer: Tan is correct. He can think: What number plus 11 makes 19? I know that 11 + 8 = 19, so the plant has grown 8 inches.

9. Tammy gives 18 markers to Penny. Penny gives 4 markers to Billy and 2 markers to Sammy. How many markers does Penny have now?
   - (A) 10
   - (B) 6
   - ● 12
   - (D) 2

Write how you know.

Possible Answer:
18−4 −2=12

10. Jill has 9 plants. She has room for 7 more plants her garden. How many plants can Jill put in her garden?

16 plants

Write how you know.

Possible Answer: I started with 9 and counted on 7 to get to 16; or I wrote a number sentence and solved it: 9+7=16.

Spectrum Test Prep Grade 1

Math 69

69

Page 70

Name _____ Date _____
Math

Solve Equations with an Unknown: Add and Subtract
Operations and Algebraic Thinking

DIRECTIONS: Answer the questions.

Strategy Balance equations by making equal quantities on both sides of the equal sign.

Test Tip The equal sign, =, means that the left side of the equation has the same value as the right side of the equation.

EXAMPLE

Which equation is true and which is false?

5 + 6 = 11

The sum of 5 and 6 is 11, so this equation is true.

5 + 4 = 3 + 7

The sum of 5 and 4 is 9. The sum of 3 and 7 is 10.

So, this equation is false, or not equal.

1. Choose the equations that are true.
   - ● 8 = 8
   - ● 9 + 1 = 5 + 5
   - (C) 12 − 4 = 5 + 7
   - ● 5 + 1 = 4 + 2

2. Write if each equation is true or false.

   14 = 6 + 8   true

   17 − 9 = 6 + 3   false

   5 + 3 = 7 + 1   true

   9 − 1 = 5 + 3   true

3. Trevor says that the equation below is not true because the first part has 3 numbers. Is Trevor correct?

   7 + 2 + 3 = 12 − 0

   No

Show how you know.

The equation is true because
7 + 2 + 3 = 12 and 12 − 0 = 12.

Test Tip Look carefully at the operation signs when you read equations.

4. What number makes each equation true? Write the number in the box.

   7 + 2 = [9]

   12 + [☐] = 13

   [7] = 16 − 9

   [10] − 2 = 8

Math 70

Spectrum Test Prep Grade 1

70

Page 71

Name _____ Date _____
Math

Solve Equations with an Unknown: Add and Subtract
Operations and Algebraic Thinking

Strategy Use addition and subtraction facts to help you balance equations. For example, 9 + 8 = 17 is the same as 17 − 9 = 8.

5. Yun had 8 apples. He and his sister ate some of the apples. Now there are 5 apples. Write an equation that shows how many apples Yun and his sister ate.

Possible Answer: 8 − ☐ = 5; or 5 + ☐ = 8

6. Solve your equation. Tell how many apples Yun and his sister ate.

Possible Answer: 8 − 3 = 5; or 5 + 3 = 8; Yun and his sister ate 3 apples.

7. Fill in the blanks. Make two true equations.

Possible Answers:
5 + 3 = 6 + 2

8 − 3 = 3 + 2

8. Write the number in the blank to make the equation true. Then, write a story problem that can be solved using the equation.

5 + _____ = 11

Possible Answer: 5 + 6 = 11; Alyssa has 11 stickers. 5 are dog stickers and the rest are cat stickers. How many cat stickers does Alyssa have? 6 cat stickers.

9. Which equations need a number greater than 6 in the blank to be true? Choose all that apply.
   - ● 13 − _____ = 5
   - ● 5 + 2 = _____
   - (C) _____ − 3 = 2
   - ● 3 + _____ = 13

Show how you know.

13 − 8 = 5; 5 + 2 = 7;
5 − 3 = 2; 3 + 10 = 13

10. Which equations need a number less than 4 in the blank to be true? Choose all that apply.
   - (A) 9 − _____ = 4
   - ● 1 + 2 = _____
   - ● _____ − 1 = 1
   - ● 3 + _____ = 4

Show how you know.

9 − 5 = 4; 1 + 2 = 3;
2 − 1 = 1; 3 + 1 = 4

Spectrum Test Prep Grade 1

Math 71

71

Page 72

Name _____ Date _____
Math

Count to 120
Number and Operations in Base 10

DIRECTIONS: Answer the questions.

Strategy Count on using ones, and then using tens for two-digit numbers. For example, counting on 3 from the number 38 is 39 (three tens, 9 ones) and 40 (4 tens and 0 ones).

Test Tip It helps to say the numbers aloud as you count.

Count on ones by writing the missing numbers in the blanks.

47 ___ 49 50 ___ ___ 54 ___ 56 ___ 58

The missing numbers in order are:
48, 51, 52, 53, 55, 57

1. Count by 1s. Fill in the missing numbers.

| 76 | 77 | 78 | 79 | 80 | 81 | 82 |

| 114 | 115 | 116 | 117 | 118 | 119 | 120 |

2. Which number is the same as the word in the box?

   five
   - ● 5
   - (B) 7
   - (C) 15
   - (D) 55

3. Here is one ◯. Draw 26 ◯.

26 circles should be drawn in the space.

◯ ◯ ◯ ◯ ◯
◯ ◯ ◯ ◯ ◯
◯ ◯ ◯ ◯ ◯
◯ ◯ ◯ ◯ ◯
◯ ◯ ◯ ◯ ◯

4. Write the number that matches the number of squares shown.

57

Math 72

Spectrum Test Prep Grade 1

72

Spectrum Test Prep Grade 1

Answer Key
119

Page 73

Count to 120
Number and Operations in Base 10

Strategy For numbers over 100, find the hundreds, tens, and ones. Say the number 523 in words: five hundreds, two tens, and three ones. Then, you can count by hundreds, tens, and ones.

Test Tip Look carefully at the operation signs when you look at equations.

5. Luka is counting his model cars. He has already counted 35 cars. He has 5 more cars to count. Which group of numbers shows how he counted the rest of his cars?
   - (A) 40, 45, 50, 55, 60
   - (B) 36, 38, 40, 42, 44
   - ● 36, 37, 38, 39, 40
   - (D) 45, 55, 65, 75, 85

6. Pedro collects sports cards. He is counting his cards by ones. He says the number "112." But, Pedro has 5 more cards to count. When he finishes counting his cards, Pedro says he has 119 cards. Is Pedro correct?

   _No_

   Show how you know.

   Possible Answer: Pedro has counted to 112, but he has 5 cards left to count. So, he can count the 5 cards: 113, 114, 115, 116, 117. Pedro has 117 cards, not 119 cards.

7. Which groups of numbers are not in the correct counting order? Choose all that apply.
   - ● 89, 88, 87, 90, 91
   - (B) 78, 79, 80, 81, 82
   - ● 89, 87, 88, 91, 92
   - (D) 79, 80, 81, 82, 83

8. Myra has 31 books on her bookshelf. Jorge has 25 books on his bookshelf. Jorge says he needs 6 more books to have the same number of books as Myra. Count by ones to see if Jorge is correct. Write the numbers on the blanks.

   25
   _26_
   _27_
   _28_
   _29_
   _30_
   _31_

   Is Jorge correct?

   Yes

73

Page 74

Understand Place Value: Tens and Ones
Number and Operations in Base 10

DIRECTIONS: Answer the questions.

Strategy Find the tens and ones in two-digit numbers. The number 78 is 7 tens and 8 ones.

Test Tip Count how many tens and then, count how many ones.

EXAMPLE

Which number shows 1 ten and 7 ones?

Tens	Ones
1	7

- (A) 1
- (B) 7
- ● 17
- (D) 71

1. Count the blocks. How many tens and ones are there?

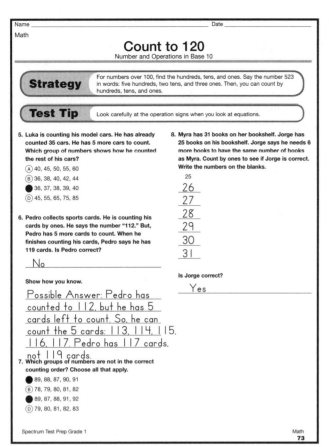

   _2_ tens   _5_ ones

2. Write the number represented by the blocks.

   _25_

3. Which number means 2 tens + 8 ones?
   - (A) 18
   - (B) 82
   - ● 28
   - (D) 8

4. How many tens and ones are in 53?
   - (A) 50 tens, 30 ones
   - ● 5 tens, 3 ones
   - (C) 3 tens, 5 ones
   - (D) 50 tens, 3 ones

5. Look at the two numbers. Are they the same or are they different?
   12   21

   different

   Write how you know.

   Both numbers have a 1 and a 2, but the first number has 1 ten and 2 ones, and the other number has 2 tens and 1 one.

74

Page 75

Understand Place Value: Tens and Ones
Number and Operations in Base 10

Strategy Use blocks, objects, or drawings to understand place value. For example, for the number 86, draw 8 boxes of tens and 6 boxes of ones.

6. What number do the blocks show?

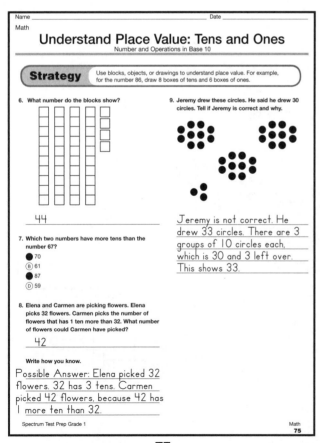

   _44_

7. Which two numbers have more tens than the number 67?
   - ● 70
   - (B) 61
   - ● 87
   - (D) 59

8. Elena and Carmen are picking flowers. Elena picks 32 flowers. Carmen picks the number of flowers that has 1 ten more than 32. What number of flowers could Carmen have picked?

   _42_

   Write how you know.

   Possible Answer: Elena picked 32 flowers. 32 has 3 tens. Carmen picked 42 flowers, because 42 has 1 more ten than 32.

9. Jeremy drew these circles. He said he drew 30 circles. Tell if Jeremy is correct and why.

   [circles drawn]

   Jeremy is not correct. He drew 33 circles. There are 3 groups of 10 circles each, which is 30 and 3 left over. This shows 33.

75

Page 76

Compare Numbers
Number and Operations in Base 10

DIRECTIONS: Answer the questions.

Strategy Compare two-digit numbers based on meanings of tens and ones digits. Identify which number is greater using tens and ones.

EXAMPLE

Compare these two numbers: 58 ____ 56.

Answer: 58 > 56

58 has 5 tens and 8 ones. 56 has 5 tens and 6 ones. They have the same number of tens, but 58 has more ones than 56. So, 58 is greater than 56.

Test Tip
< means less than
> means greater than
= means equal to

Which number is less than 71? Choose the best answer.
- ● 70
- (B) 73
- (C) 84
- (D) 92

1. Adia jumped rope for 43 seconds. Zahra jumped rope for 46 seconds. Who jumped rope for more seconds?

   Zahra

   Write how you know.

   I compared the numbers. 46 is greater than 43, so Zahra jumped for more seconds.

2. Hector is 51 inches tall. Rudy is 55 inches tall. Write <, >, or = to compare how tall the boys are.

   51 _<_ 55

3. Write two numbers between 46 and 56. Then, tell which number is greater and why.

   Possible Answer: 48 and 54; 54 is greater than 48 because 54 has 5 tens, and 48 has only 4 tens.

4. Compare the numbers. Write <, >, or = in the ☐.

   65 [>] 61
   31 [=] 31
   58 [<] 85
   26 [<] 28

76

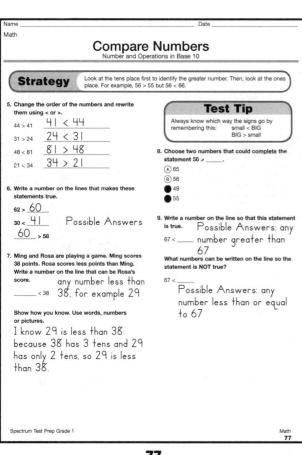

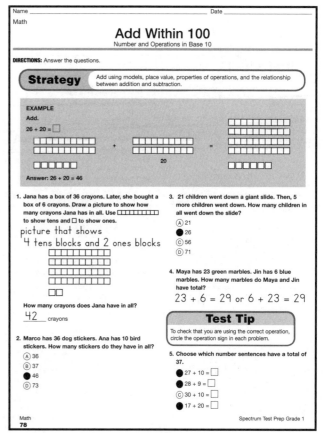

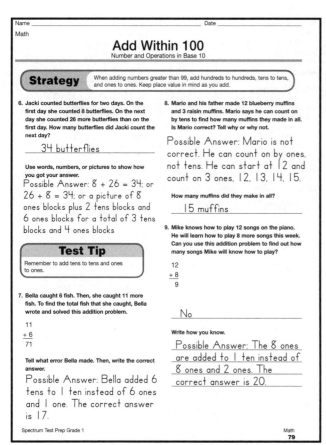

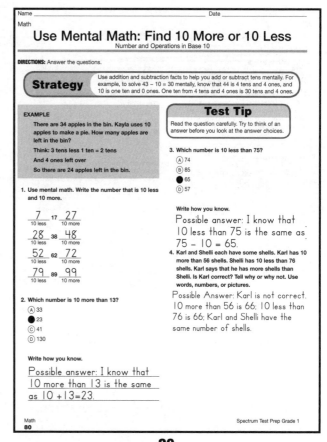

Use Mental Math: Find 10 More or 10 Less
Number and Operations in Base 10

Strategy Read each problem carefully and look for words that tell you if you are looking for *how many more* or *how many less*.

5. Dawn and Kelly have 10 more notebooks than Matt and Laura. Matt and Laura have 25 notebooks.

Dawn and Kelly have 5 notebooks. They used this number sentence 25 – 10 = 5.

Is this correct? Tell why or why not. Use words, numbers, or pictures.

6. Gino has 25 pennies. He spends 10 pennies at the store. How many pennies does Gino have left?

__15__ pennies

How do you know?

Possible Answer: I know that 10 less than 25 is 15. So, Gino has 15 pennies left.

7. 67 children are at the park. 10 more children come to the park. How many children are at the park now? Choose the best answer.
- (A) 77 ●
- (B) 76
- (C) 57
- (D) 68

Write how you know.

Possible answer: I know that 10 more than 67 is the same as 10 + 67 = 77.

Test Tip

Read the directions carefully. This will keep you from making simple mistakes and having to redo your work.

8. Choose the two statements that are true.
- (A) 56 is 10 more than 66.
- ● 87 is 10 less than 97.
- (C) 23 is 10 more than 32.
- ● 41 is 10 less than 51.

9. Tam has 56 points in a game. This is 10 less points than Shara has. How many points does Shara have?

__66__ points

Write how you know.

Possible answer: I know that 10 less than 56 is the same as 56 + 10 = 66.

81

Subtract Multiples of 10
Number and Operations in Base 10

DIRECTIONS: Answer the questions.

Strategy Think out the problem in your head using place value to solve it mentally. For example, think *40 plus what number makes 50*? 4 plus 1 makes 5, so 40 plus 10 makes 50. This helps you solve 40 – ☐ = 50.

EXAMPLE
There are 40 cows in the field. 20 cows go to the barn. How many cows are still in the field?
Think:
40 – 10 = 30
30 – 10 = 20
Answer: There are 20 cows still in the field.

1. Fill in the missing number to complete each number sentence.
80 – 10 = __70__
60 – 30 = __30__
70 – 20 = __50__
50 – 40 = __10__

2. Erik wrote an answer of 30 for a subtraction problem. Choose the two problems that Erik could have solved.
- ● 50 – 20
- (B) 30 – 10
- ● 80 – 50
- (D) 40 – 30

Write how you know.

Possible answer: I know that 50–20=30 and 80–50=30.

3. Ali has 60 trading cards. She gives Garrett 20 of them. How many trading cards does Ali have left?

__40__

Show how you know. Use words, numbers, or pictures.

Possible Answer: I thought 20 plus what number makes 60? I know that 2 plus 4 makes 6, so 20 plus 40 makes 60. Ali has 40 trading cards left.

Test Tip

Knowing subtraction facts can help you subtract tens mentally.

4. What is the difference of 80 and 60?
- (A) 10
- ● 20
- (C) 30
- (D) 40

Write how you know.

Possible answer: I know that 80-60=20.

5. What is another way to show 70 – 40 = 30?

Possible Answer: 80-50=30; 50-20=30

82

Subtract Multiples of 10
Number and Operations in Base 10

Strategy Use place value to identify which numbers are greater. Identify the tens and ones, remembering that tens are always greater than ones.

6. Grant's coach has 40 baseballs at the beginning of the baseball season. Grant's team loses 20 of them at practice and 10 of them during games. How many baseballs does Grant's coach have at the end of the season?

__10__

Write how you know.

Possible answer: I know that 40 –20–10=10.

7. Emma bought 40 balloons for a party. On the way home, 10 balloons popped. Write and solve a subtraction sentence to find how many balloons were left.

__40__ – __30__ = __10__ balloons

8. Kyle says that the difference of 50 – 20 is greater than the difference of 5 – 2. Is Kyle correct?

Yes

Write how you know.

Possible answer: 50 – 20 = 30 and 5 – 2 = 3; 30 is greater than 3 because 3 tens are greater than 3 ones.

9. Choose the two number sentences that have a difference of 30.
- (A) 50 – 30 = ☐
- (B) 30 – 30 = ☐
- ● 70 – 40 = ☐
- ● 90 – 60 = ☐

10. Lauren has 60 tomato plants. Lindsay has 40 tomato plants. How many more plants does Lauren have? Show your work. Use numbers, words or pictures.

Possible Answer: Lauren has 20 more plants than Lindsay. Student may draw 6 tens rods and cross out 4 to show subtracting 4 tens from 6 tens to make 2 tens or 20; or a number sentence: 60 – 40 = 20

11. Choose the two number sentences that have a difference of 40.
- ● 90 – 50 = ☐
- (B) 40 – 10 = ☐
- (C) 50 – 20 = ☐
- ● 60 – 20 = ☐

12. Amanda says that the difference of 80 – 40 is greater than the difference of 8 – 4. Is Amanda correct?

Yes

Write how you know.

Possible answer: 80 – 40 = 40 and 8 – 4 = 4; 40 is greater than 4 because 4 tens are greater than 4 ones.

83

Order and Compare Lengths
Measurement

DIRECTIONS: Choose the best answer.

Strategy Order and compare lengths indirectly by using a third object.

EXAMPLE
Compare how tall the football players are. Who is taller, Player A or Player B?

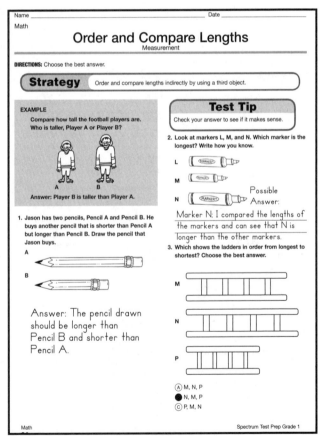

Answer: Player B is taller than Player A.

1. Jason has two pencils, Pencil A and Pencil B. He buys another pencil that is shorter than Pencil A but longer than Pencil B. Draw the pencil that Jason buys.

A

B

Answer: The pencil drawn should be longer than Pencil B and shorter than Pencil A.

Test Tip

Check your answer to see if it makes sense.

2. Look at markers L, M, and N. Which marker is the longest? Write how you know.

L

M

N

Possible Answer:
Marker N; I compared the lengths of the markers and can see that N is longer than the other markers.

3. Which shows the ladders in order from longest to shortest? Choose the best answer.

M

N

P

- (A) M, N, P
- ● N, M, P
- (C) P, M, N

84

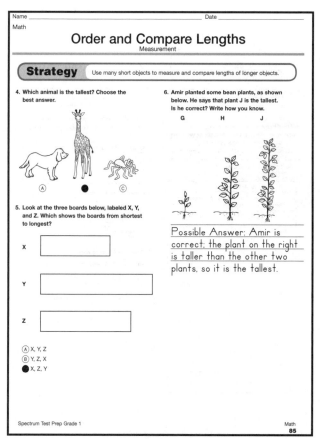

Name _____ Date _____
Math

Order and Compare Lengths
Measurement

Strategy Use many short objects to measure and compare lengths of longer objects.

4. Which animal is the tallest? Choose the best answer.

(A)   ● (B)   (C)

5. Look at the three boards below, labeled X, Y, and Z. Which shows the boards from shortest to longest?

X

Y

Z

(A) X, Y, Z
(B) Y, Z, X
● X, Z, Y

6. Amir planted some bean plants, as shown below. He says that plant J is the tallest. Is he correct? Write how you know.

G   H   J

Possible Answer: Amir is correct; the plant on the right is taller than the other two plants, so it is the tallest.

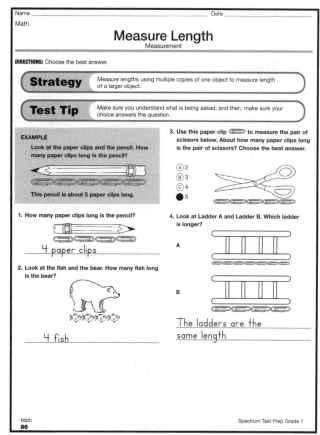

Name _____ Date _____
Math

Measure Length
Measurement

DIRECTIONS: Choose the best answer.

Strategy Measure lengths using multiple copies of one object to measure length of a larger object.

Test Tip Make sure you understand what is being asked, and then, make sure your choice answers the question.

EXAMPLE
Look at the paper clips and the pencil. How many paper clips long is the pencil?

This pencil is about 5 paper clips long.

1. How many paper clips long is the pencil?

4 paper clips

2. Look at the fish and the bear. How many fish long is the bear?

4 fish

3. Use this paper clip to measure the pair of scissors below. About how many paper clips long is the pair of scissors? Choose the best answer.

(A) 2
(B) 3
(C) 4
● 5

4. Look at Ladder A and Ladder B. Which ladder is longer?

A

B

The ladders are the same length.

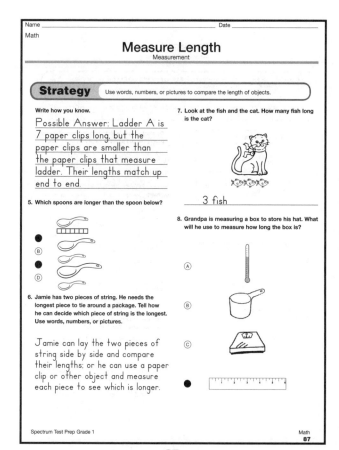

Name _____ Date _____
Math

Measure Length
Measurement

Strategy Use words, numbers, or pictures to compare the length of objects.

Write how you know.

Possible Answer: Ladder A is 7 paper clips long, but the paper clips are smaller than the paper clips that measure ladder. Their lengths match up end to end.

5. Which spoons are longer than the spoon below?

● (A)
(B)
(C)
(D)

6. Jamie has two pieces of string. He needs the longest piece to tie around a package. Tell how he can decide which piece of string is the longest. Use words, numbers, or pictures.

Jamie can lay the two pieces of string side by side and compare their lengths; or he can use a paper clip or other object and measure each piece to see which is longer.

7. Look at the fish and the cat. How many fish long is the cat?

3 fish

8. Grandpa is measuring a box to store his hat. What will he use to measure how long the box is?

(A)

(B)

(C)

●

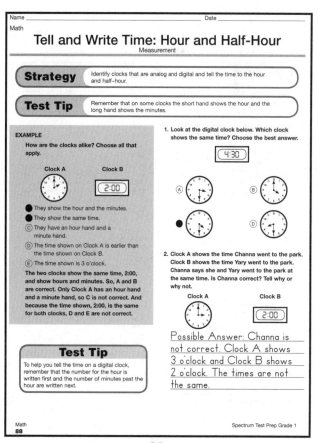

Name _____ Date _____
Math

Tell and Write Time: Hour and Half-Hour
Measurement

Strategy Identify clocks that are analog and digital and tell the time to the hour and half-hour.

Test Tip Remember that on some clocks the short hand shows the hour and the long hand shows the minutes.

EXAMPLE
How are the clocks alike? Choose all that apply.

Clock A   Clock B
               2:00

● They show the hour and the minutes.
● They show the same time.
(C) They have an hour hand and a minute hand.
(D) The time shown on Clock A is earlier than the time shown on Clock B.
(E) The time shown is 3 o'clock.

The two clocks show the same time, 2:00, and show hours and minutes. So, A and B are correct. Only Clock A has an hour hand and a minute hand, so C is not correct. And because the time shown, 2:00, is the same for both clocks, D and E are not correct.

Test Tip
To help you tell the time on a digital clock, remember that the number for the hour is written first and the number of minutes past the hour are written next.

1. Look at the digital clock below. Which clock shows the same time? Choose the best answer.

4:30

(A)   (B)

●   (D)

2. Clock A shows the time Channa went to the park. Clock B shows the time Yary went to the park. Channa says she and Yary went to the park at the same time. Is Channa correct? Tell why or why not.

Clock A   Clock B
               2:00

Possible Answer: Channa is not correct. Clock A shows 3 o'clock and Clock B shows 2 o'clock. The times are not the same.

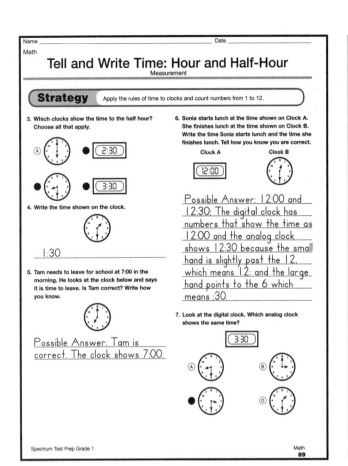

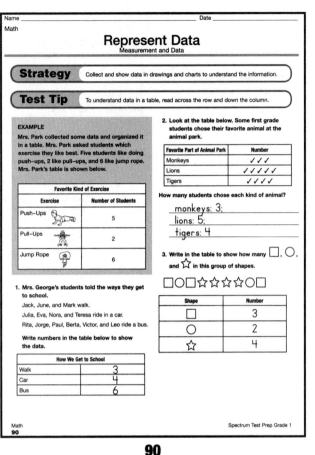

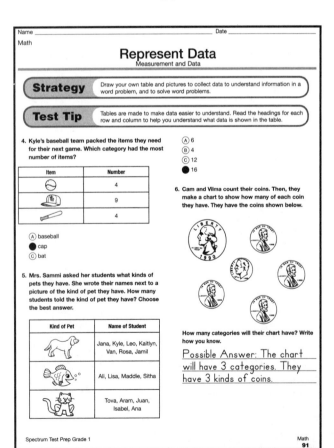

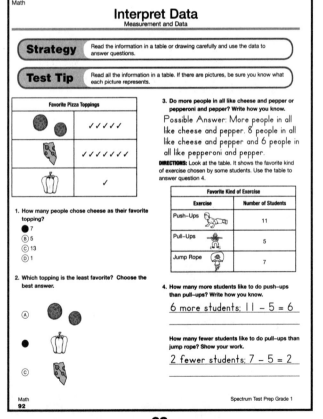

Interpret Data
Measurement and Data

Strategy Read the top of each column to find out what kind of information is given in a table. Then, read the directions for each table carefully to know what information to find.

DIRECTIONS: Look at the table. It shows some students' favorite part of the animal park. Each ✓ = 1 student. Use the table to answer questions 5, 6, and 7.

Favorite Part of Animal Park	Number
Monkeys	✓✓✓
Lions	✓✓✓✓✓
Tigers	✓✓✓✓

5. How many students in all liked the lions and the tigers best? How do you know?

Possible Answer: 9 students; I counted the check marks, 5 for lions and 4 for the tigers, to make 9.

6. Which two animals were chosen by less than 5 students?
● monkeys
Ⓑ lions
● tigers

7. Which two animals were chosen by more than 3 students?
Ⓐ monkeys
● lions
● tigers

DIRECTIONS: Look at the chart. Mr. Samson asked some of his students how they get to school each day. They wrote their names on the chart next to how they get to school. Use the chart to answer questions 8 – 10.

How We Get to School	
Bus	Janice, Jon, Geraldo, Kim
Car	Marcos, Noel, Rita
Bike	Rosa, Jason, Felipe, Angela, Tran

8. How many students in all rode the bus or a bike?

9 students

9. How many fewer students rode in a car than a bus?

1 student

10. How many students in all rode the bus or in a car?

7 students

93

Identifying Attributes of Shapes
Reason with Shapes and Their Attributes

Strategy Learn and understand defining attributes and non–defining attributes of shapes to identify shapes of objects.

Test Tip A defining attribute is a feature that applies to a shape, such as number of corners, number of edges, or if the edges are straight or curved. A non–defining attribute can apply to any shape, such as color and size.

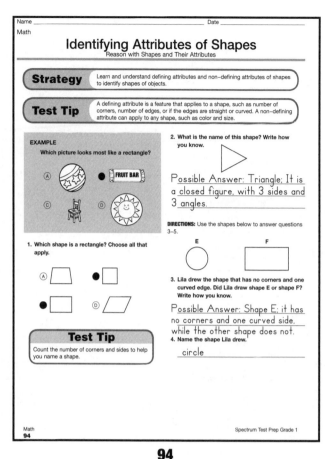

EXAMPLE
Which picture looks most like a rectangle?

Ⓐ ● FRUIT BAR Ⓒ Ⓓ

1. Which shape is a rectangle? Choose all that apply.

Ⓐ ●

● Ⓓ

Test Tip
Count the number of corners and sides to help you name a shape.

2. What is the name of this shape? Write how you know.

Possible Answer: Triangle; It is a closed figure, with 3 sides and 3 angles.

DIRECTIONS: Use the shapes below to answer questions 3–5.

E   F

3. Lila drew the shape that has no corners and one curved edge. Did Lila draw shape E or shape F? Write how you know.

Possible Answer: Shape E; it has no corners and one curved side, while the other shape does not.

4. Name the shape Lila drew.

circle

94

Identifying Attributes of Shapes
Reason with Shapes and Their Attributes

Strategy Sort shapes into groups by identifying the attributes, or features, that are the same.

5. Tell why the other shape cannot be the shape Lila drew.

Possible Answer: Shape F is a rectangle. It has 4 corners and straight sides.

6. Draw a square inside a triangle.

Possible Answer:

DIRECTIONS: Gayle wants to sort these shapes into groups. Use the shapes to answer questions 7–10.

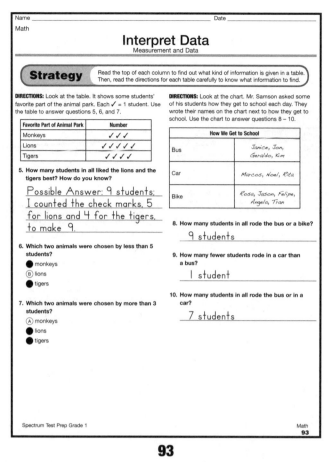

Test Tip
Look carefully at the attribute of a shape. Even though the colors, sizes, or positions of one type of shape are different, the kind of shape does not change if it has the same number of corners and sides.

7. Gayle put all the circles in one group. How many circles are in the group?

6

8. How many shapes have stripes? Name the shapes.

4; square, triangle, circle

9. How many shapes are white triangles?

3

10. How many shapes are white?

7

11. Choose the answer that describes the shape below.

Ⓐ round with no corners
● four corners with straight sides
Ⓒ three corners with curved sides
Ⓓ one corner with round side

12. Describe a circle in your own words.

Possible Answer: round, no corners, one curve

95

Compose Composite Shapes
Reason with Shapes and Their Attributes

Strategy Create composite shapes from two–dimensional and three–dimensional shapes. Use sketches to help you visualize the new shape.

Strategy A composite shape is a new shape made by combing multiple shapes, such as making a rectangle with two squares.

EXAMPLE
Which shape was used to make this shape?

Ⓐ ● Ⓒ Ⓓ

1. What shapes will you have if you cut this shape in half? Choose the best answer.
Ⓐ two circles
● two squares
Ⓒ two rectangles
Ⓓ two triangles

Test Tip
Imagine what each object looks like before choosing your answer.

2. Choose the shapes that can be combined to make a square.
● Ⓑ

● Ⓓ

3. Nona said the shape below is a cube. Is Nona correct? Tell why or why not.

Possible Answer: Nona is not correct; the shape is a cylinder. A cylinder has a curved edge and two circle faces; a cube has no straight edges and square faces.

4. What three-dimensional shapes were used to make this new figure? Choose all that apply.

●
Ⓑ
●
●

96

Compose Composite Shapes
Reason with Shapes and Their Attributes

Strategy Identify the attributes of single shapes that make up a composite figure. For example, does the shape have a round or straight edge? Flat or circle face?

5. Draw a new figure using these three shapes.

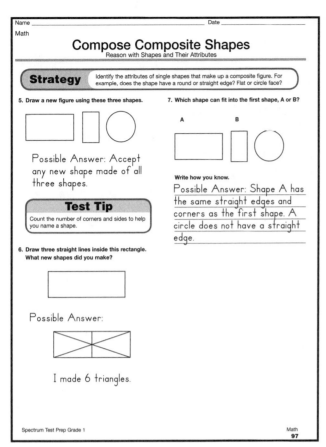

Possible Answer: Accept any new shape made of all three shapes.

Test Tip
Count the number of corners and sides to help you name a shape.

6. Draw three straight lines inside this rectangle. What new shapes did you make?

Possible Answer:

I made 6 triangles.

7. Which shape can fit into the first shape, A or B?

A   B

Write how you know.
Possible Answer: Shape A has the same straight edges and corners as the first shape. A circle does not have a straight edge.

97

Partition Shapes into Equal Shares
Reason with Shapes and Their Attributes

Strategy Understand that a whole is made up of two halves, four fourths, or four quarters and apply the rules of wholes to answer questions.

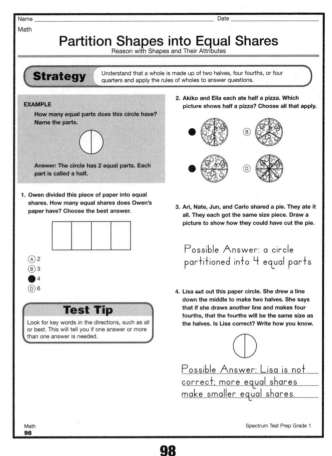

EXAMPLE
How many equal parts does this circle have? Name the parts.

Answer: The circle has 2 equal parts. Each part is called a half.

1. Owen divided this piece of paper into equal shares. How many equal shares does Owen's paper have? Choose the best answer.

Ⓐ 2
Ⓑ 3
● 4
Ⓓ 6

Test Tip
Look for key words in the directions, such as all or best. This will tell you if one answer or more than one answer is needed.

2. Akiko and Ella each ate half a pizza. Which picture shows half a pizza? Choose all that apply.

3. Ari, Nate, Jun, and Carlo shared a pie. They ate it all. They each got the same size piece. Draw a picture to show how they could have cut the pie.

Possible Answer: a circle partitioned into 4 equal parts

4. Lisa cut out this paper circle. She drew a line down the middle to make two halves. She says that if she draws another line and makes four fourths, that the fourths will be the same size as the halves. Is Lisa correct? Write how you know.

Possible Answer: Lisa is not correct; more equal shares make smaller equal shares.

98

Partition Shapes into Equal Shares
Reason with Shapes and Their Attributes

Strategy Ask yourself how many parts equal a whole to answer questions about dividing shapes into equal parts.

Test Tip In questions that are grouped together, look for information in one question that may help you answer another.

5. Toby wants to equally share a fruit bar with Alan. He cuts the bar into 2 pieces as shown below.

Will Toby and Alan each get an equal share? Tell how you know.
Possible Answer: Yes, they will each get an equal share. The bar is divided into 2 equal parts.

6. Name each part of the bar.
Each part of the bar is one-half.

7. How can Toby make another cut in the bar so he can share it equally with 2 more friends? Draw a picture to show your answer.

Possible Answer: a drawing that shows another diagonal drawn to divide the bar into 4 equal size pieces

8. On Monday, David and his sister shared a small pizza. It was cut into 2 equal-size pieces. On Saturday, David shared the same-size pizza with three of his friends. This pizza was cut into 4 equal-size pieces. Did David eat more pizza on Monday or on Saturday? How do you know? Use words or pictures.

Possible Answer: David ate more pizza on Monday, because a one-half share is bigger than a one-fourth share. A drawing can also show that one-half is larger than one-fourth.

99

Strategy Review

In this section, you will review the strategies you learned and apply them to practice the skills.

Strategy Use basic operations to solve problems.

EXAMPLE
There are 3 cows, 4 horses, and 7 sheep in the field. How many animals are there in all in the field?
First, write a number sentence. Use a ☐ for the unknown number.
$3 + 4 + 7 = ☐$
Next, change the order of the addends to make groups that are easy to add, like 3 and 7.
$3 + 7 + 4 = ☐$
Now, add 3 + 7.
$3 + 7 = 10$
Then, add 10 + 4.
$10 + 4 = 14$
The number of animals in all is 14.

1. The sum of 7 + 6 is the same as the sum of _____. Choose three.
● 3 + 3 + 7
● 6 + 7
● 2 + 5 + 6
Ⓓ 7 + 8

2. Jana saw 9 ants in a line. 4 ants marched into their ant hill. Write a number sentence to show how to find how many ants are left. Then, solve it. Use a ☐ for the number of ants that are left.
$9 - 4 = ☐$;
5 ants are left.

3. Hal solved this problem by writing and solving an addition number sentence.
Ina has 14 sports cards. She gives 5 sports cards to Aaron.
How many sports cards does Ina have left?
Complete the number sentence to show how Hal solved the problem. Then, write how many sports cards Ina has left.
$\underline{9} + 5 = 14$
Ina has $\underline{9}$ sports cards left.

4. Jan has 12 marbles. Gayle gives her 7 more. Jan and Gayle each write a number sentence to find how many marbles Jan has all together.
Jan's Way: $12 + 7 = ☐$ marbles
Gayle's Way: $7 + 12 = ☐$ marbles
Which way is correct? Write how you know.
Possible Answer: Both ways are correct. The order of the addends does not matter.

5. Solve each number sentence, and tell how many marbles Jan has all together.
$12 + 7 = 19$; $7 + 12 = 19$; Jan has 19 marbles.

100

Answer Key
126

Spectrum Test Prep Grade 1

Strategy Review

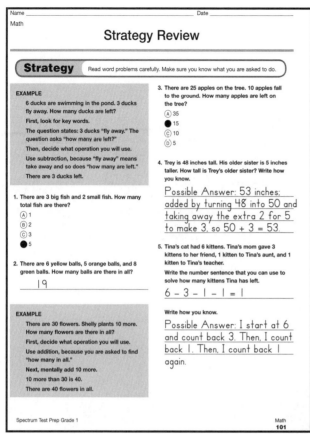

Strategy   Read word problems carefully. Make sure you know what you are asked to do.

EXAMPLE

6 ducks are swimming in the pond. 3 ducks fly away. How many ducks are left?

First, look for key words.

The question states: 3 ducks "fly away." The question asks "how many are left?"

Then, decide what operation you will use.

Use subtraction, because "fly away" means take away and so does "how many are left."

There are 3 ducks left.

1. There are 3 big fish and 2 small fish. How many total fish are there?
   Ⓐ 1
   Ⓑ 2
   Ⓒ 3
   ● 5

2. There are 6 yellow balls, 5 orange balls, and 8 green balls. How many balls are there in all?
   ___19___

EXAMPLE

There are 30 flowers. Shelly plants 10 more. How many flowers are there in all?

First, decide what operation you will use.

Use addition, because you are asked to find "how many in all."

Next, mentally add 10 more.

10 more than 30 is 40.

There are 40 flowers in all.

3. There are 25 apples on the tree. 10 apples fall to the ground. How many apples are left on the tree?
   Ⓐ 35
   ● 15
   Ⓒ 10
   Ⓓ 5

4. Trey is 48 inches tall. His older sister is 5 inches taller. How tall is Trey's older sister? Write how you know.

   Possible Answer: 53 inches; added by turning 48 into 50 and taking away the extra 2 for 5 to make 3, so 50 + 3 = 53.

5. Tina's cat had 6 kittens. Tina's mom gave 3 kittens to her friend, 1 kitten to Tina's aunt, and 1 kitten to Tina's teacher.
   Write the number sentence that you can use to solve how many kittens Tina has left.

   6 - 3 - 1 - 1 = 1

   Write how you know.

   Possible Answer: I start at 6 and count back 3. Then, I count back 1. Then, I count back 1 again.

101

Strategy Review

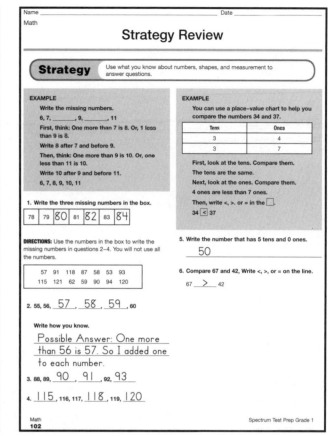

Strategy   Use what you know about numbers, shapes, and measurement to answer questions.

EXAMPLE

Write the missing numbers.

6, 7, _____, 9, _____, 11

First, think: One more than 7 is 8. Or, 1 less than 9 is 8.

Write 8 after 7 and before 9.

Then, think: One more than 9 is 10. Or, one less than 11 is 10.

Write 10 after 9 and before 11.

6, 7, 8, 9, 10, 11

1. Write the three missing numbers in the box.

78	79	80	81	82	83	84

DIRECTIONS: Use the numbers in the box to write the missing numbers in questions 2–4. You will not use all the numbers.

57	91	118	87	58	53	93
115	121	62	59	90	94	120

2. 55, 56, __57__, __58__, __59__, 60

   Write how you know.

   Possible Answer: One more than 56 is 57. So I added one to each number.

3. 88, 89, __90__, __91__, 92, __93__

4. __115__, 116, 117, __118__, 119, __120__

EXAMPLE

You can use a place-value chart to help you compare the numbers 34 and 37.

Tens	Ones
3	4
3	7

First, look at the tens. Compare them.

The tens are the same.

Next, look at the ones. Compare them.

4 ones are less than 7 ones.

Then, write <, >, or = in the ☐.

34 < 37

5. Write the number that has 5 tens and 0 ones.

   __50__

6. Compare 67 and 42. Write <, >, or = on the line.

   67 __>__ 42

102

Strategy Review

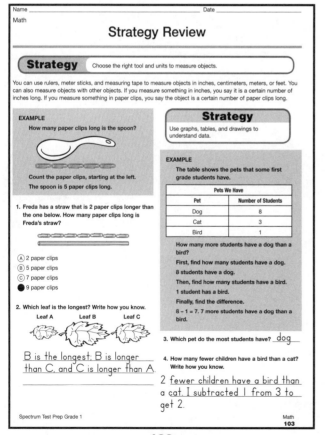

Strategy   Choose the right tool and units to measure objects.

You can use rulers, meter sticks, and measuring tape to measure objects in inches, centimeters, meters, or feet. You can also measure objects with other objects. If you measure something in inches, you say it is a certain number of inches long. If you measure something in paper clips, you say the object is a certain number of paper clips long.

EXAMPLE

How many paper clips long is the spoon?

Count the paper clips, starting at the left.

The spoon is 5 paper clips long.

1. Freda has a straw that is 2 paper clips longer than the one below. How many paper clips long is Freda's straw?

   Ⓐ 2 paper clips
   Ⓑ 5 paper clips
   Ⓒ 7 paper clips
   ● 9 paper clips

2. Which leaf is the longest? Write how you know.

   Leaf A   Leaf B   Leaf C

   B is the longest; B is longer than C, and C is longer than A.

Strategy

Use graphs, tables, and drawings to understand data.

EXAMPLE

The table shows the pets that some first grade students have.

Pets We Have	
Pet	Number of Students
Dog	8
Cat	3
Bird	1

How many more students have a dog than a bird?

First, find how many students have a dog.

8 students have a dog.

Then, find how many students have a bird.

1 student has a bird.

Finally, find the difference.

8 – 1 = 7. 7 more students have a dog than a bird.

3. Which pet do the most students have? __dog__

4. How many fewer children have a bird than a cat? Write how you know.

   2 fewer children have a bird than a cat. I subtracted 1 from 3 to get 2.

103
